Probate

A straightforward guide
to obtaining a grant of probate
and administering an estate

. . . .

Regina Meizoso LLB ACA

About the Author

Regina Meizoso read Law at Exeter University. After graduating she trained and qualified as a Chartered Accountant with PricewaterhouseCoopers, one of the largest accountancy firms in the world.

She is authorised by the Institute of Chartered Accountants in England and Wales to provide non-contentious probate services in England and Wales.

IMPORTANT INFORMATION: Exclusion of Liability and Disclaimer

Contents

Contents

Preface

If you are reading this book you are probably one of the many thousands of people every year who are faced with sorting out the affairs of someone who has died. The majority of you will be first timers with no real knowledge of what is involved and a sense of uncertainty about what to do next.

This publication is designed to help you help yourself by providing you with the knowledge required to make informed choices and decisions about what lies ahead. You may very well be able to undertake the entire process yourself, with no or minimal advice from a solicitor or professional advisor; the reality is many thousands of people every year do just this and save themselves significant amounts of money.

We recommend you read the complete book before you begin; it will take a few hours, enable you to get your bearings, and provide you with an overview of the journey ahead. Appendix 2 sets out a to-do list by chapter to help you along the way. It is not possible to cover every situation. And so, if you come across anything at all that you have doubts about or feel unsure of, you should consider seeking professional advice. We have included a list of circumstances where you should definitely consult an appropriately qualified individual in Chapter 2.

And finally, you should be aware that this book only relates to estates situated in England and Wales and that the law is different in other countries. If the deceased owned assets located outside England and Wales, you will need to consult a solicitor qualified in the law of the relevant country to help you deal with those specific items.

An introduction to legal jargon

There are words and phrases which we will use regularly throughout this book but are seldom used in everyday language. You can find their meaning within the glossary. Here, we briefly introduce the more commonly used words and phrases which are helpful to know about right from the start.

The person who has died is the deceased. At the time of death, the deceased may have owned assets such as a house, bank accounts, a car and so on. The deceased may also have owed unpaid debts and bills such as a mortgage, loans, utility bills, etc. Everything that the deceased owned and owed at the date of death is referred to as the 'estate' or 'death estate'. The process of sorting out the deceased's estate is known as 'administering the estate'.

The person or people responsible for administering the estate are called personal representatives and there are two types; executors and administrators. Executors are those individuals named in a valid will. Administrators are those individuals appointed by the law if no executors are named within the will, no named executor within the will is prepared or able to act, or there is no valid will.

Whilst administering the estate, the personal representative may need to apply for a legal document called a 'grant of representation', more commonly known as 'probate'. This document gives the personal representative the legal authority to deal with certain assets held in the deceased's name including property, bank accounts and shares.

There are three types of grant of representation, all of which have the same application procedure. The one required depends on the circumstances. We describe each below.

1. *A grant of probate.* This is issued when the deceased left a valid will with named executors who are willing and able to act.

2. *A grant of letters of administration (with will annexed).* This is issued when there is a valid will but no executor is named within it or none of the named executors are prepared or able to act.

3. *A grant of letters of administration.* This is issued where the deceased did not leave a valid will.

The grant of representation is issued by one of the many probate registries located across the country. The registries themselves are part of the court system in England and Wales.

Finally, the word 'probate' is often used to describe administering the estate as a whole although, strictly speaking, should only be used to refer to the application made for a grant of representation.

We are now ready to move onto the first step of administering an estate – identifying who the personal representatives are and who, therefore, has the authority to act.

1. Who can administer an estate?

1.1.   Setting the scene

Before you begin to administer an estate, you need to identify who is legally responsible for doing so. Is it you?

Broadly speaking, if you are named as an executor in a valid will left by the deceased then you are entitled to administer the estate. If no executors are named within the will or no named executor is prepared or able to take on the responsibility, then the beneficiaries of the will have the right to do so. If the deceased did not leave a valid will then close relatives of the deceased have the authority to act.

1.2.   Where a valid will exists

The law says executors named within a valid will are given first priority to act as personal representatives, however, an executor is under no obligation to accept appointment. There are two possible options available to the reluctant executor.

If he or she does not wish to act they can outright refuse by 'renouncing' their right. This is irrevocable (you cannot change your mind later on), and so they must be sure this is what they want. Renouncing can be actioned by notifying the probate registry.

If the executor chooses to renounce their right they must do so before they undertake any action relating to administering the estate, otherwise known as 'intermeddling'. Put simply, if someone starts the job they must finish it!

Chapter 1: Who can administer an estate?

The sale of property, the payment and collection of debts and running the deceased's business has been classed as intermeddling in the courts. Attending to funeral arrangements, ensuring the deceased's dependants are looked after and safeguarding the deceased's property by moving it to a safe place is not intermeddling.

If an executor decides that they do not wish to act as a personal representative at the current time but may wish to do so at some stage in the future, they can choose to 'reserve power'. This effectively leaves the door open by allowing them to apply later on if they should need or wish to. This might prove useful if problems arise with administering the estate down the line. Again, this can be actioned by notifying the probate registry.

If no named executor is able or prepared to act, or the will does not name an executor, then the law gives beneficiaries of the deceased's estate the right to act as an administrator in the following order:

1. Those entitled (holding in trust for another person) to the residuary estate. The residuary estate is the part of the estate which remains after the payment of all funeral and legal expenses, debts and legacies.

2. Those entitled to the residuary estate or, where the residue is not wholly disposed of by the will, any person entitled to share in the undisposed of residue.

3. The personal representative of those entitled to the residuary estate (but not one for life, or one holding in trust for another person), or the personal representative of any person entitled to share in any residue not disposed of by the will.

4. Any other beneficiary of the will or any creditor of the deceased.

5. The personal representative of any other beneficiary of the will (but not one for life or one holding in trust for any other person), or the personal representative of any other creditor of the deceased.

No group will be considered for appointment until the entire preceding group is confirmed as not being willing or able to act.

1.3.   Where a valid will does not exist

If the deceased did not leave a valid will, the legal order of entitlement to act as an administrator is as follows:

1. Spouse or civil partner of the deceased.

2. Child or issue of a child who predeceased the deceased.

3. Father or mother of the deceased.

4. Brothers and sisters of the whole blood (i.e. sharing both parents) or issue of brothers and sisters of the whole blood who predeceased the deceased.

5. Brothers and sisters of the half-blood (i.e. sharing one parent) or issue of brothers and sisters of the half-blood who predeceased the deceased.

6. Grandparents.

7. Uncles and aunts of the whole blood or issue of uncles and aunts of the whole blood who predeceased the deceased.

8. Uncles and aunts of the half-blood or issue of uncles and aunts of the half-blood who predeceased the deceased.

9. The Crown.

10. Creditors of the deceased.

The above includes legitimate and illegitimate children but not stepchildren. Any claimant must have a beneficial interest and all claimants within each group are equally entitled. A grant of representation will not be given to members of one class jointly with another.

1.4.   Executor or administrator – why does it matter?

Executors and administrators are both personal representatives. Their duties are essentially the same but the distinction between the two matters from a legal point of view.

An executor derives their power from the will itself and is therefore able to act as a personal representative from the date of the deceased's death. An administrator must obtain a grant of representation in order to have the legal authority to act and cannot deal with the deceased's assets until the date this is issued.

1.5.   Age and number of personal representatives

Any person can be appointed as an executor or administrator provided they are not lacking in mental capacity or bankrupt. However, a person under the age of 18 cannot obtain a grant of representation. If a minor is one of several executors, power can be reserved until he or she reaches the age of 18 and the grant will be issued to the co-executors. If a minor is the sole executor, a limited grant can be made on his or her behalf by an adult.

A will can name any number of executors. The probate registry will, however, only accept a maximum of four to obtain a grant of representation. The others may reserve their power. Likewise, only a maximum of four administrators may apply for a grant of representation.

2. Plan ahead...before you begin

2.1. Setting the scene

This chapter covers a few areas which are useful to know about and consider before you begin the main work of administering the estate. Giving these matters some thought now will help you to get organised and focus your thinking. At times, we briefly touch upon topics which are covered in more detail in later chapters.

2.2. Do I want to be a personal representative and what is involved?

Being a personal representative is a position of great responsibility which carries with it a risk of personal financial liability if errors are made. You must act in good faith, not abuse your position and act reasonably and honestly at all times. The position is for life and does not terminate once the estate is finalised. The appointment as a personal representative should not be taken lightly.

You may decide to appoint a professional advisor to represent you, or to do the work yourself, or a mixture of both. However, regardless of the path you end up taking you will still need to spend time making telephone calls, writing letters, finding documents, attending meetings and signing relevant paperwork. You should, therefore, make a realistic appraisal of your time before committing to the role.

2.3. What is a grant of representation and do I need one?

A grant of representation, more commonly known as 'probate', is the document which proves the legal authority of the personal representative to act. It is issued by one of the many probate registries located across the country. You select which probate registry to use when making the application for a grant of representation.

Many organisations, for instance certain banks and other financial institutions, will need to see the grant of representation before they allow the personal representative access to the deceased's assets. The assets to which the grant of representation applies are frozen until this time.

Not all estates require a grant of representation. Certain low value estates do not; neither do estates which are made up entirely of joint assets which pass automatically to the surviving joint owner.

The application process for obtaining a grant of representation involves deciding which probate registry to use, completing an application form, assembling and providing the requested supporting documentation, paying a fee and attending an interview to swear an oath. All personal representatives who wish to be named on the grant of representation must attend the interview. In straightforward cases, it can typically take four weeks from the date the application is submitted to the probate registry for a grant of representation to be issued.

More detail on the different types of grant, which assets require a grant and the process generally can be found in Chapter 11.

2.4.   How long does administering an estate take?

There is no 'one size fits all' answer to this question. All estates are different and have their own challenges and timescales varying anywhere between a couple of months to a year or more. The following list includes some of the factors which may influence how long it takes.

❖ Determining the number and complexity of assets and debts which make up the estate and whether the associated paperwork is organised and clear.

❖ Establishing the existence and whereabouts of any final will and whether there are any concerns as to its validity or interpretation.

❖ The number of external organisations which need to be informed of the death and the efficiency of their customer service and internal processes.

❖ The efficiency and effectiveness of any appointed professional advisors.

❖ Establishing asset valuations and agreeing those valuations with HMRC.

❖ Organising the funding and payment of any inheritance tax bill.

❖ The length of time taken to sell certain assets, for example, a house.

❖ The complexity of the deceased's personal tax position.

❖ Whether a grant of representation is needed.

❖ Any dispute or claim brought by an interested third party.

Take a moment to consider how these factors might apply to your situation and what impact they may have on timings.

2.5.   Do I need a solicitor?

If you undertake an online search for probate services you will be met with a variety of choices. Broadly speaking, these fall into four categories.

1. The 'do it yourself' option where you purchase a kit or book. Some publications offer a telephone helpline or e-mail support for a set period of time at an additional cost.

2. The 'grant only' option where providers offer to complete the probate registry and HMRC paperwork for you, usually for a fixed fee. Again, some offer a telephone helpline or e-mail support for a set period of time.

3. The 'as and when' service where you consult a professional advisor when you need help on specific points only.

4. The fully managed probate service. Here, providers undertake the whole estate administration process from start to finish for either a fixed fee or hourly rate. Some may charge a percentage of the value of the estate on top of their fee.

The 'do it yourself' option may be suitable if the estate is relatively straightforward and you have the time and motivation to administer the estate; thousands of people every year do just this and save themselves significant amounts of money. And remember, HMRC and HM Courts and Tribunals Services provide a wealth of free information and a helpline to deal with tax and grant queries. Details are available on the government website.

If you do decide to use an advisor, make sure they are regulated by an approved body such as the Solicitors Regulation Authority or the ICAEW. This means they must meet certain professional standards and have a complaints procedure in place. They will also have appropriate insurance cover to give you peace of mind in the event that they make a mistake as a result of their negligence. In terms of fees charged, it is always worth shopping around. Do bear in mind that, as with anything, cheapest isn't necessarily best. Remember, you can save money by doing some of the more mundane work yourself and leaving the trickier areas to a professional.

The circumstances where it is strongly advisable to seek professional advice include the following:

❖ The terms of the will are not clear or there are grounds to suppose the will is invalid.

❖ The estate, or part thereof, passes to children under the age of 18.

❖ Trusts are involved.

❖ The deceased owned assets abroad, for example, shares, property or bank accounts.

❖ The deceased owned a business or agricultural property.

❖ Anyone is likely to dispute the will.

❖ The estate is insolvent i.e. the value of debts exceeds the value of assets.

❖ The estate is of insufficient value to pay all legacies due.

❖ The inheritance tax calculations are complex, or there is likely to be a significant inheritance tax bill and there is a possibility of reducing the amount.

❖ A deed of variation is required.

❖ Beneficiaries cannot be located or the deceased died without leaving a will and there is a question mark over who or where the beneficiaries are.

❖ The deceased made a significant number of gifts and lifetime transfers in the seven years before they died.

❖ The personal representative is unclear about any point.

You should always seek professional advice if a problem arises that you feel unable to deal with.

2.6. Is there enough money in the estate to pay all debts?

If there is not enough money to pay all debts, the estate is said to be insolvent. The law gives a set order in which debts should be paid in this circumstance and any errors on the part of the personal representative may result in personal liability. You may wish to consider renouncing your right to act as personal representative altogether if this applies.

2.7. Finding the money to pay inheritance tax

If the deceased's estate is likely to have an inheritance tax liability, you will need to think ahead and ensure you have funds available to pay the amount due. The deadline for payment of inheritance tax is six months after the end of the month in which the death occurred or when you submit the HMRC tax form, whichever is earlier. Interest is charged from this time and the rate at the time of publication is 3%.

A grant of representation will not be issued until any inheritance tax bill is settled. This could prove a problem if you need to use assets which are the subject of the grant of representation as payment. The following is a series of options potentially open to you if this is the case. Do bear in mind that they take time to arrange and so some forward planning is required.

❖ If the deceased owned NS&I products, these may be used to satisfy all or part of any inheritance tax due. This can take up to four weeks to arrange. Details are available on the NS&I website.

❖ Under the 'Direct Payment Scheme', a bank or building society will release funds to HMRC to settle inheritance tax due. Details are available on the government website. You will need to check whether the deceased held any accounts with banks or building societies which are part of the scheme. If so, contact each organisation and ensure you understand their requirements well in advance of payment having to be made.

❖ Inheritance tax can be paid in ten equal annual instalments on certain assets. Interest is chargeable on all outstanding amounts and any late payments. You may pay by instalments on land and buildings, certain shares and securities, the net value of a business or interest in a business, and timber. One of the more common assets where inheritance tax is paid by instalments is the deceased's main residence. Inheritance tax must be paid in full if the asset is sold.

❖ You may wish to consider taking out a bridging loan to cover any inheritance tax due. The interest charged is an expense of the estate.

2.8.   The hidden costs of administering an estate

It is worth spending a moment outlining the other costs which may arise when administering an estate. Ultimately, these costs will be borne by the estate provided there are sufficient funds available. You may, however, have to find temporary funding where costs are payable in advance of a grant of representation being issued.

❖ The cost of making an application for a grant of representation without a solicitor is £215 for estates with a value of more than £5,000.[1]

❖ The fees for copies of the death certificate and grant of representation.

❖ The fees for statutory notices to protect the personal representative from any unknown claims made on the estate.

❖ Any fees payable to valuation experts, e.g., chartered surveyors, jewellers, stockbrokers, etc., in order to obtain asset valuations for HMRC purposes.

❖ Any fees payable to tax accountants assisting with finalising the deceased's tax position and the position of the deceased's estate.

All of these areas are covered in later chapters.

---

[1] This is correct at the time of publication. The government has, however, recently withdrawn proposals for the introduction of a new fee scale based on estate values which would have significantly increased fees for certain estates from May 2017.

Finally, the next of kin or family and friends are normally responsible for organising the funeral and meeting the funeral expenses, although the responsibility can fall to a personal representative named in the will. If this is the case, then check the following.

❖ Did the deceased have a pre-paid funeral plan or funeral insurance?

❖ If there are sufficient funds in the deceased's bank account, make enquiries with the relevant bank to see if they are prepared to release funds to the personal representative. The larger banks and building societies will normally agree to do so subject to paying the funeral director directly.

❖ Is it possible to use funds from a bank account held jointly by the deceased and another individual?

❖ Does the funeral director offer an instalment payment plan option?

We have now come to the end of our section on planning ahead. The remaining chapters of this book take you through the practical matters associated with being a personal representative and administering an estate beginning with registration of the death.

3. Register the death

3.1. Setting the scene

When a person dies, a doctor signs and issues a medical certificate stating the cause of death together with a leaflet explaining who is eligible to register the death. It is usual for a family member to register the death although the responsibility may fall to the personal representative if there is no surviving family able or available to do so.

3.2. Registering the death

The death should be registered at a register office within five days of death unless a coroner's report is required in which case the death cannot be registered until the relevant paperwork is received from the coroner's office. The signed medical certificate, together with the following paperwork where available, should be presented to the registrar.

- ❖ Birth certificate
- ❖ Driving licence
- ❖ Passport
- ❖ Marriage certificate
- ❖ National insurance number
- ❖ Proof of address

Once the death is registered, you will receive the 'Green Form' giving permission for burial or cremation, Form BD8 (benefits agency certificate) and a death certificate. Using the register office local to where the death occurred will normally result in receiving the paperwork on the same day as registration, otherwise you may have to wait for a few days and burial may be delayed as a result. You may need to make an appointment to attend the registry.

3.3.   Death certificate and copies

It is worth obtaining a number of copies of the death certificate as you will need to send it to several organisations when notifying the death. It speeds up the administration process if you have a few copies to hand so you can contact several organisations at the same time. It is cheaper to obtain copies at the time of registration rather than after the event.

3.4.   The 'Tell Us Once' scheme

The register office may offer you the 'Tell Us Once' scheme whereby you can request certain governmental agencies are notified of the death, in one go, directly by the registrar. You will be provided with a leaflet outlining the details. This service is only available in certain counties.

4. Safeguard and protect estate assets and pets

4.1. Setting the scene

Personal representatives are responsible for safeguarding and protecting the assets of the estate. They may be held personally liable if any property is lost, stolen or destroyed and the estate is worth less as a result. You must, therefore, give this area your immediate attention and make it a priority.

4.2. Practical steps

Any property and moveable personal chattels belonging to the deceased such as cars, jewellery, clothing, furniture and so on, should be physically secured or moved to safe, secure storage. If a property is unoccupied, consider turning off the utilities and also think about the danger of any water pipes freezing and act accordingly. If several people or parties have access to the property, consider whether it is necessary to change the locks or entry security codes.

You need to arrange appropriate insurance cover for assets which have none. For existing insurance policies, read the documents and make sure the cover is adequate and all conditions are being met. Existing insurers should be notified as soon as possible of the change in circumstances. This includes the providers of any house and contents insurance. If the deceased owned a motor vehicle, the insurance should be amended to third party, fire and theft and the vehicle secured off road with the appropriate road tax licence.

4.3.   Witnesses and recording visits

It is preferable to have a third-party present as a witness when making visits to the deceased's property and moving portable items in order to avoid any possible allegations of theft and misappropriation. You should record the details of your visits and ask the witness to sign and date the paperwork. If you have a camera capable of date stamping, or a video recording facility such as a smartphone, this is also useful for recording visits.

4.4.   Pets

If the deceased had pets, ensure that suitable arrangements are in place to safeguard their welfare. The will (if any) may let you know the deceased's wishes with regard to pets. Otherwise, the RSPCA, Dog's Trust and Blue Cross all have rehoming facilities in the event that no friends or family members are able to take responsibility.

5. Establish who is entitled to inherit

Part 1: If there is a will

5.1.   Setting the scene

If the deceased left a will, the personal representative is responsible for checking it meets certain legal requirements and making sure the estate is distributed in accordance with the deceased's instructions. This duty can be difficult to carry out if the will is complicated, poorly drafted or unclear in any way, so make sure you seek legal advice if you have any doubts about the areas we are about to cover, or there is anything at all that you do not understand or is not addressed below.

The deceased (known as the 'testator' when talking about the will) may have also left a codicil (or several codicils) in addition to the original will. A codicil is a formal document that amends rather than replaces a will, and is read together with the will. We refer to wills below but the same measures should be applied to codicils.

5.2.   Locating the original will

It is self-evident that before you can check and interpret any will you must first find it. It is really important that any will you have in your possession is the original document rather than a copy. It must also be the last valid will made by the testator. If you can only find a copy of the will, and not the original, contact the probate registry who can provide guidance on what to do next. If you do find a will then further searches should be made to ensure there are no later wills.

❖ The earlier the date of the will the higher the likelihood the will is out of date and changes have been made.

The most obvious place to begin looking for a will is in the deceased's home and amongst their personal paperwork. You can also ask the deceased's professional advisors, e.g., bankers, accountants, solicitors and so on, if they are aware of the existence of a will. If you find a Certificate of Deposit when searching through the deceased's paperwork, this means the will is kept at the Principal Registry of the Family Division in London and you should contact them to reclaim it. Even if you cannot find a Certificate of Deposit, it is worth making enquiries at the Principal Registry. They keep an index of wills which is searched each time an application for a grant of representation is made.

The deceased may have registered their will with an online commercial organisation such as the National Will Register (or 'Certainty' as it is otherwise known). They provide a will registration and search service for a fee and can also ask solicitors, in the area where the deceased lived, whether they hold the deceased's will.

5.3. Keeping the will safe…some practical considerations

It is really important that the physical condition of the original will is not compromised. If there is any sign of tampering, the probate registry may challenge its validity when you come to apply for a grant of representation. You must also safeguard the physical document itself. Try and remember the following:

❖ Do not attach any additional documents to the original will using staples, paperclips or any other type of adhesive.

❖ Never remove any documents from the original will or take the original will apart for any purpose.

❖ Never write on, or annotate, the original will.

❖ Keep the original will in a secure place.

❖ Make a copy of the original will without taking the document apart in any way. Keep the copy separate from the original will.

❖ Always use a safe and secure method of transport when sending the original will to relevant parties such as the probate registry or a solicitor, e.g., recorded delivery, courier, by hand, etc.

5.4.   **What makes a will valid?**

The will itself must follow certain legal requirements in order to be considered valid, otherwise it will fail. The probate registry takes a close look at the will as part of the grant application process to make sure it meets these legal requirements, which we list below. Carefully check the document you have in your possession to make sure it complies.

❖ The will is in writing.

❖ The will is signed by the testator or by someone in his presence and at his request.

❖ The testator's signature is witnessed by two persons who are present together when the testator signs the will.

❖ The witnesses have each signed the will in the presence of the testator.

❖ The testator is 18 years of age.

The will should also be dated at the time of execution.

A will usually contains an attestation clause. This clause tells us that the formalities regarding witnesses, as noted above, have been met. It appears next to the testator's signature immediately above the witnesses' signatures and typically reads as follows:

'Signed by the testator in our presence and attested by us in the presence of the testator and of each other.'

The signatures of the testator and witnesses should appear at the end of the will. Any requirements or wishes which follow on from the signatures can indicate additional information was added after the will was signed. If this is the case, the probate registry will require witnesses to swear an affidavit confirming the words were present at the time of signature.

In addition to the above, the testator must have been mentally capable in law of making a will, otherwise it is invalid. This means the testator, <u>at the time of making the will</u>, had:

❖ A rough understanding of what a will is.

❖ A rough idea of their property.

❖ An understanding of who would benefit from the will and who they had a moral obligation to benefit (even if they chose not to).

❖ An understanding of the effect of the will.

A person can have the legal capacity to make a will in spite of suffering from a mental disorder provided the mental disorder did not affect the above conditions <u>at the time of making the will</u>.

Finally, a will must have been made of the testator's own free will and free from the duress of others, otherwise it is invalid.

5.5.   Privileged wills

Privileged wills can be oral or written and do not need to comply with legal requirements. They can be made by a member of HM Forces engaged in actual military service or in conditions similar to actual military service. Other personnel (as defined by law) engaged in conditions similar to actual military service may also make privileged wills.

5.6.   Has the will been cancelled or altered?

A will may be cancelled (the legal term for this is 'revoked') in a number of ways. If a will is revoked it means it is no longer valid and fails. The following is a list of ways in which a will may be revoked.

❖ *By a new will or codicil, either expressly or impliedly.* A new will expressly revokes an earlier will by including a clause saying so. This may read something like *'I hereby revoke all former wills and testamentary dispositions made by me and declare this to be my last valid will'.* If a new will does not contain such a clause, then the new will only revokes a previous will to the extent that it is inconsistent with the terms of the earlier will. It is, therefore, possible to have two valid wills.

❖ *By destruction.* The will may be revoked simply by the testator destroying it, or by directing its destruction, which must be done in the presence of the testator. In either case the destruction must be intended to revoke the will.

❖ *By marriage or civil partnership.* If the testator marries or forms a civil partnership, any existing will is automatically revoked unless the testator expressly states in the will that it is made in contemplation of marriage to, or forming a civil partnership with, a particular person.

A will may also be revoked partially through divorce or nullity, or cessation of a civil partnership. This causes a bequest to a former spouse or civil partner, or their appointment as an executor, to fail unless there is a clearly expressed contrary intention. It is possible for the failed beneficiary to challenge this position and bring a claim under The Inheritance (Provision for Family and Dependants) Act 1975. This is covered in more detail in Chapter 14.

If a will has been altered, any amendment must follow the legal formalities required for preparing the will. If this has not happened, and the original words remain legible, a court will revert to this original wording. If both the original wording and the amended words are not legible, a court will ignore both.

5.7.   Wills containing foreign property

If a will contains property situated abroad, such as a holiday home, it is recognised as valid under English law provided it meets the legal requirements of the law of the state where the property is situated. It is advisable to consult a lawyer qualified to practise in the relevant state if this applies. The probate registry may require an affidavit from an expert in the relevant foreign law.

5.8.   Wills made outside England and Wales

If a will is made outside England and Wales, it is accepted as valid under English law provided it meets the formalities of the state where it was made and, at the date of the will, the testator was domiciled in, habitually resided in or was a national of that state.

5.9.   The reasons why bequests fail

The following are instances where a bequest made within a will is, or may be, void. Look out for these when reading the will and seek professional advice if required.

❖ A bequest to a former spouse or civil partner, or their appointment as an executor, fails through divorce, nullity or cessation of a civil partnership. This is subject to any clearly expressed contrary intention.

❖ A witness, or the spouse or civil partner of a witness, cannot benefit under a will unless there are two other independent witnesses. A bequest made to such an individual will be void. The remainder of the will is not affected. If, however, an attesting witness marries or enters into a civil partnership with a beneficiary after the date of the will, this does not invalidate the bequest.

❖ Bequests contrary to public policy may be void. The meaning of public policy changes over time although includes conditions that weaken the family unit or affect the choice of one's religion.

❖ Bequests which breach the rules against perpetuities and accumulation. This is a complex area of law designed to prevent bequests being accumulated over an excessive period of time and made to beneficiaries whose identity will not be known for a number of years in the future, e.g., any future grandchildren not yet born.

❖ Irreconcilable bequests whereby two clauses in a will contradict each other. There is a general rule that, if two parts of a will are inconsistent with each other, the later clause should succeed and the earlier fail, however, this is not set in stone.

❖ Bequests to beneficiaries who have predeceased the testator, or organisations which no longer exist, fail. There are exceptions to the rule. The most common is where a bequest in a will to a child or remoter issue of the testator does not lapse if the dead beneficiary leaves children who are alive at the testator's death. This does not apply where a contrary intention is shown in the will.

❖ Bequests of property which the testator does not own. A bequest is not voided if a separate bequest is also made to the actual owner of the property and accepted.

❖ Uncertain bequests may fail if the wording of the will is not clear as to what is being left or to whom it is being left, e.g., *'some of my collection of china dolls to one of my daughters'* would fail.

❖ A bequest is conditional and the condition fails.

❖ There are insufficient assets to pay debts. If there are insufficient assets to settle all debts the estate is said to be insolvent. If this is the case, all bequests fail.

❖ There are insufficient assets to pay the bequest.

5.10. A specific item gifted in the will no longer exists

If a specific item gifted in a will no longer exists at the date of death, the gift may fail. A careful reading of the will is required to establish whether the gift is described in enough detail to separately identify it with absolute certainty. If it is, then the gift is classed as specific and fails. If the gift is described in broad, general terms then it may still be valid.

As an example, *'I give Anne my mother's gold bracelet'* is described in a very specific way with no doubt about which gold bracelet the testator is referring to. If this gold bracelet no longer exists at the time of death, the gift fails and the intended beneficiary receives nothing.

On the other hand, if the will reads *'I give Anne a gold bracelet',* then any gold bracelet will do. This gift does not fail and could be satisfied by either a gold bracelet from the estate (if one exists) or a gold bracelet purchased by the personal representative.

It is possible for a gift to partially fail if a part of it is sold prior to death. If, for example, 1,000 ABC Plc shares are specifically bequeathed within a will and only 600 of those shares remain at the date of death, those 600 remaining shares pass under the will. The balance of 400 shares fails.

If the will states that a gift is to be paid from a specific source of funds which no longer or only partially exists at the date of death, the gift may be funded from other estate assets. As an example, *'I give Bob £500 from my HSBC bank account'* can be funded from the remaining estate assets if the HSBC bank account no longer exists or contains less than £500. However, if the will reads *'I give Bob the funds in my HSBC bank account',* the bequest fails if the specific bank account no longer exists.

Finally, you must check the will carefully for any clause which entitles the beneficiary of the failed gift to receive a replacement, or the proceeds from any sale of the gift which took place before death.

5.11. Ambiguous or meaningless clauses

If a will contains words or clauses which are unclear or make no sense, a court can look at evidence of the testator's intention to try and bring meaning and clarity. If the court is unable to do so, the purported bequest made by the relevant wording fails. Legal advice should be sought if this applies.

5.12. Corrections to a will

A court may order the correction of a will in two circumstances. Firstly, if a clerical error has been made, e.g., a bequest intended to be £10,000 is incorrectly stated as £100. Secondly, where the person who prepared the will failed to understand the testator's instructions, e.g., a solicitor misunderstands the testator's instruction to leave property to Anne, and drafts the will to leave property to Bob instead. Seek legal advice if these circumstances apply.

5.13. Bequests which are always exempt from inheritance tax

Bequests made to a spouse or civil partner, qualifying charities and other UK national organisations as defined by HMRC, are always exempt from inheritance tax regardless of any clause in the will.

Part 2: If there is no will

5.14. Setting the scene

When a person dies without leaving a valid will they are said to die intestate and their estate is distributed according to a set of laws known as the intestacy rules. A person may die partially intestate if they fail to include all of their property in their will. If this is the case, the personal representative(s) must distribute the estate in accordance with both the valid will and the intestacy rules.

We outline the intestacy rules which apply to deaths from 1 October, 2014, below. The rules are different for deaths which occurred before this time. In all cases, the estate is distributed after payment of taxes and debts. You will see the rules make no allowances for cohabitees or stepchildren, neither of whom have any entitlement.

5.15. Scenario 1: Married couples and civil partnerships with children

If a married couple or civil partnership have children, the surviving partner will take the following:

❖ The first £250,000 tax free plus interest from the date of death until payment at the Bank of England rate.

❖ Personal chattels of the deceased (defined as anything that is not monetary, business assets or 'held as investment')

❖ Half of what remains (known as 'the remainder').

The children will receive, in equal shares, half of anything above £250,000. 'Children' include both adopted and illegitimate children but not stepchildren. If any of the children are minors, their entitlement is only conditional and must be held in trust until they reach the age of 18, or enter into a marriage or civil partnership if earlier.

If a child has died before the deceased parent and left their own child or children (i.e. grandchildren of the deceased), the child or children will automatically take their parent's share by substitution in equal shares.

5.16. Scenario 2: Married couples and civil partnerships, no children

For married couples and civil partnerships without children, provided the spouse or civil partner outlives the deceased by 28 days, he or she will inherit the estate.

5.17. Scenario 3: No surviving spouse or civil partner

Where there is no surviving spouse or civil partner (including where a spouse or civil partner dies within 28 days of the deceased), the entire estate goes to the nearest group of relatives in equal shares. If all members of a group of relatives have died before the deceased, the next group inherits. The groups, in order of entitlement, are as follows:

1. Children or their descendants.

2. Parents.

3. Brothers and sisters of the whole blood (sharing both parents) or their descendants.

4. Brothers and sisters of the half-blood (sharing one parent) or their descendants.

5. Grandparents.

6. Uncles and aunts of the whole blood or their descendants.

7. Uncles and aunts of the half-blood or their descendants.

8. The Crown, Duchy of Lancaster or Duke of Cornwall.

If a beneficiary next in line to inherit within groups 1, 3, 4, 6 or 7 dies before the deceased, their descendants (if any) will automatically take their parent's share equally by substitution. The legal term for this is 'per stirpes'.

5.18. The beneficiary is under 18 years of age

The groups numbered 2, 5 and 8 in scenario 3 above inherit any entitlement they may have absolutely (i.e. unconditionally). For all other categories, any inheritance is conditional upon them reaching the age of 18 or entering into a marriage or civil partnership before they reach the age of 18. When they do so, they will inherit absolutely. Until then their inheritance is contingent and must be held in trust. In legal terms, their inheritance is subject to what is known as the 'statutory trusts'.

5.19. Intestacy rules: an example

Here is an example to demonstrate how the intestacy rules operate.

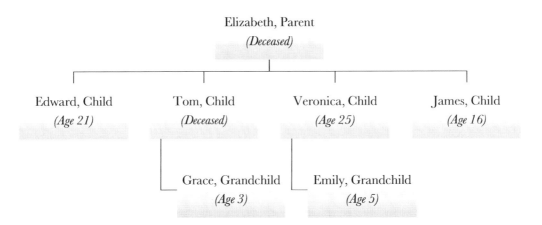

Elizabeth, a widow, dies intestate. Her husband died a number of years ago and she has four children one of whom, Tom, predeceased her. Her estate will be divided into four. Veronica and Edward will be entitled to their share absolutely because they have reached the age of 18. Tom's share will pass 'per stirpes' to his child Grace. Both James and Grace only have a contingent interest in the estate at this point and their entitlement is subject to the statutory trusts. They must wait until they reach the age of 18, or enter into a marriage or civil partnership if earlier, to inherit. If they die before this their share will be divided between Elizabeth's surviving children. Emily receives no interest in Elizabeth's estate as her mother, Veronica, is still alive.

The same rationale would apply if groups 3, 4, 6 or 7 listed in scenario 3 were in line to be beneficiaries of an intestate estate.

Part 3: Joint assets

5.20. Establishing the legal position: joint tenants and tenants-in-common

Property, for example, houses, land, banks accounts and so on, can be held jointly in one of two ways under English law. It is important to know which way applies as this tells us how the item is treated when one of the owners dies. We explain each below. Note that the word 'tenant' has nothing to do with renting a property, which is what one might naturally assume.

1. *Joint tenants:* If the property is owned as joint tenants, the deceased's share automatically passes to the survivor regardless of any clause in their will or the intestacy rules.

2. *Tenants-in-common:* If the property is owned as tenants-in-common, the deceased's share passes under the terms of their will or intestacy rules.

We provide more information on how to find out the type of joint ownership for specific assets in Chapter 6.

Part 4: Changing the entitlement: deeds of variation

5.21. Can the inheritance be varied by the beneficiaries?

Beneficiaries may seek to vary their inheritance after the deceased's death. This may be desirable for a number of reasons such as obtaining a better tax position. A deed of variation is required to give effect to any changes and must be executed within two years of death. The deed only affects inheritance tax and capital gains tax and does not change the general law or income tax position. Professional advice should be sought if this is in point.

6. Identify and value the estate

Part 1: General

6.1.   Setting the scene

We shall now turn our minds to the task of gathering information relating to the deceased's affairs and valuing the estate. This includes details of all assets held in both sole and joint names as well as any trust assets from which the deceased benefitted. Details of outstanding debts are also required together with the value of any gifts the deceased made within seven years of death.

Certain items are only relevant for calculating inheritance tax and do not form part of the deceased's estate distributed to beneficiaries under the will or intestacy rules. For instance, assets owned as joint tenants pass directly to the surviving owner regardless of any clause in a will or the intestacy rules. The personal representative does not have to deal with these assets, however, the value of the property is still chargeable to inheritance tax and must be reported to HMRC.

6.2.   What type of information should I be looking for?

Undertake a thorough search of the deceased's paperwork and online affairs to identify any information which might help to finalise the estate's affairs such as:

❖ Banks statements and cheque books

❖ Tax returns

❖ NS&I paperwork

- ❖ Utility and other bills

- ❖ Share certificates

- ❖ Pension statements

- ❖ Car registration documents

- ❖ Mortgage papers and statements

- ❖ Insurance policies

- ❖ Payslips

- ❖ Lease or tenancy agreements

- ❖ Trust deeds

Additionally, make enquiries of close family and friends, as well as the deceased's solicitor, accountant, stockbroker and financial advisors.

You need to keep a list of all assets, debts and gifts you come across when searching through the deceased's affairs. There are suggested worksheet formats in Appendix 3 for this purpose.

6.3. What value should I use?

The estate must be valued at open market value at the date of death for HMRC purposes. This means the realistic selling price not, for instance, insurance or replacement value. Going forward, the open market value will be used as the base cost of the asset for capital gains tax purposes. We provide more detail on valuing individual types of assets throughout the chapter.

6.4. Can I estimate the value of assets?

Potentially. If the deceased's estate meets the criteria for completing the HMRC Form IHT 205, and the gross value of the estate before deducting debts is below £250,000, then you may choose to estimate the value of assets. You may also estimate the value of the estate if the criteria for completing HMRC Form IHT 205 is met and the estate passes to a spouse, civil partner or qualifying charity. HMRC forms are discussed in Chapter 10.

Obtaining professional valuations can be expensive and so estimating values may save money. However, any estimate must be supported by sound and suitable evidence. Be aware that HMRC may challenge any valuations, particularly if the estate is paying inheritance tax or is close to the threshold for doing so.

Part 2: Specific assets, debts and gifts

6.5. Land and buildings

Land and buildings includes:

❖ The deceased's home and any rental investment properties

❖ Farms

❖ Business property, e.g., hotels, shops, factories

❖ Timber and woodlands

❖ Other land and buildings, e.g., lock-up garages, redundant or derelict land

❖ Other rights that attach to land, e.g., fishing or shooting rights

You must first establish whether the property is held in the deceased's sole name or jointly (either as joint tenants or tenants-in-common). If the property is unregistered, locate the title deeds and check for evidence of ownership rights. For registered land, download the Title Register from the Land Registry website. The name of any joint owners will be given on the document and the following wording, or similar, will appear if the property is held as tenants-in-common:

'No disposition by a sole proprietor of the registered estate (except a trust corporation) under which capital money arises is to be registered unless authorised by an order of the court'.

Once you have confirmed how the property is owned, you must establish the open market value at the date of death. HMRC requires details of the full value together with a calculation of the deceased's share. For jointly held property, they allow a 10% deduction in value from the deceased's share if the surviving owner is not a spouse or civil partner. This may be increased to 15% if the surviving owner is occupying the property.

❖ The capital gains tax implications of claiming this deduction should be carefully considered.

The valuation of land and buildings can be complicated and, in many cases, you will need to use the services of an estate agent or chartered surveyor for which a fee will be payable. If you obtain several valuations, adopt the mid-range but make sure you understand the reasons for any significant fluctuations. Offers received to purchase any property should also be taken into account when forming an opinion.

Where the estate is likely to incur inheritance tax, the valuation will be checked by the district valuer from HMRC who may challenge it. If the property is sold soon after obtaining a grant of representation, the district valuer may seek to substitute the valuation given for the sales price achieved.

❖ If the property is registered, check the Title Register of the property with the Land Registry to establish ownership rights. Doing this will help avoid making any mistakes with the HMRC and probate forms, or the distribution of the asset.

❖ A property can be marketed for sale prior to obtaining a grant of representation. This may result in an earlier sale if so desired. However, ownership cannot be legally transferred until the grant is received. You should make all relevant parties (e.g., estate agents, buyers, solicitors, etc.) aware of the situation if you decide to proceed down this route.

6.6.   Motor vehicles

Valuations for motor vehicles can be obtained either through a local garage or through various websites, e.g., Auto Trader. Remember to include any additional value for private licence plates if applicable.

6.7.   Household and personal goods

Household and personal goods includes furniture, pictures, paintings, china, TVs, audio and video equipment, cameras, cars, caravans, jewellery, boats, antiques, stamp collections and so on.

HMRC say no professional valuation is required for ordinary household items whose individual value is less than £500 and there is no requirement to individually list such items. Online searches of auction resale sites such as e-Bay may be useful in establishing a value. Keep supporting evidence for any estimates you make yourself.

For individual items with a value of over £500, HMRC strongly advise a professional valuation be undertaken.

If you must or choose to have a professional valuation, consider using an auctioneer and request the value of items if sold by auction on the date of death. Valuations of jewellery should be requested from a jeweller. Fees will apply.

Certain awards are exempt from inheritance tax including awards for service in the armed forces and those made by the State in recognition of public life.

❖ HMRC may challenge valuations, particularly if the level of household contents appears low given the deceased's living arrangements or circumstances.

❖ Home insurance policies may pinpoint certain high value possessions owned by the deceased, although the insurance value is not the same as open market value.

❖ Take photographs of items. This might prove useful in the event of a challenge by HMRC.

6.8. Cash and bank accounts

Banks and building societies with whom the deceased held an account should be notified of the death as soon as possible. The relevant organisation will freeze the deceased's account until either a grant of representation has been issued or it is confirmed that a grant of representation is not required. All direct debits, standing orders and unpresented cheques will be stopped, as well as any access to funds.

The valuation of bank and building society accounts is straightforward. The open market value is the balance of the deceased's share at the date of death together with any interest due but not yet paid. The relevant organisation will provide you with this. You must also include the value of any spare cash belonging to the deceased.

In terms of jointly held accounts, the majority will be held as joint tenants. There are, however, circumstances where an account may be held as tenants-in-common or, in substance, solely. For instance, if an account was held in joint names for convenience only and all funds were provided by the deceased, then the full amount should be included within the deceased's estate.

❖ If you suspect the deceased may have held bank or building society accounts for which you have no details, try searching www.mylostaccount.org.uk. It is a free service provided by the British Bankers' Association, the Building Societies Association and NS&I. You can apply online or by post if you prefer.

6.9.   National Savings and Investments (NS&I)

The NS&I website provides a comprehensive guide to the process for dealing with the deceased's investments. You must complete Form NS&I 904, gather the requested paperwork, and send it to the address given. A grant of representation is not always required to gain access to funds where the total of the deceased's investments do not exceed £5,000, although this is at the discretion of NS&I.

NS&I will provide the value of investments for inclusion in the death estate.

Premium bonds can either be repaid or remain in each prize draw for up to 12 months following death. Any prizes must be distributed in accordance with the will or intestacy rules.

❖ If you suspect the deceased may have held NS&I products but do not have details, again try searching www.mylostaccount.org.uk. Alternatively, you can use NS&I's tracing service by downloading and completing a form from their website and sending it to the address as directed.

❖ You can access monies from NS&I in advance of obtaining a grant of representation to pay for funeral director expenses and inheritance tax. Organise this as soon as possible if required. Details are on the NS&I website.

6.10. Stocks and shares

Begin by compiling a list of shareholdings owned by the deceased at the date of death including the number, name, nominal value and type of share, for instance, '*75 ABC plc £1 Ordinary Shares*'. Once done, contact the share registrar for each of the companies (or the deceased's stockbroker if applicable) to notify the death and verify the holdings are correct.

Next, find the value of quoted stocks and shares at the date of death in the financial section of a newspaper such as the Financial Times. You will need a newspaper dated the day following death as values given on any particular day are always for the day before. The Historic Price Service at www.londonstockexchange.com can also provide a value for a small fee. Your local public library may also hold the information. Look out for share prices marked *'XD (Ex-div)'*. This means a dividend is due on the share but has not yet been paid. If this is the case, the value of this dividend must be added to the share price.

Once you have the values, HMRC's guidance notes for completing Forms IHT 205 and IHT 400 (discussed in Chapter 10) provide a clear and comprehensive guide to valuing the total shareholding owned.

Alternatively, rather than undertaking the task yourself, you can use a share valuing service, stockbroker or fund manager to value quoted shareholdings. A fee will be payable which you should confirm in advance.

For shares held in unquoted investments, contact the company secretary of the relevant company in the first instance to request a valuation.

❖ The deceased's paperwork and bank statements may provide clues as to the existence of any shareholdings. Look out for dividend or interest income paid directly into their bank account, evidence of tax vouchers, invitations to Annual General Meetings or correspondence with stockbrokers. The deceased may have kept share certificates at home or with their bank, solicitor or stockbroker.

❖ It is not unusual for share certificates to be mislaid. If you cannot locate share certificates, you may be asked by the relevant company to sign a statutory declaration and indemnity before selling or transferring legal ownership. This protects the company from any future claims in the event that the share certificates are found and the claimant is not the beneficiary. A fee will be charged if this is required.

6.11. Businesses

If the deceased owned a business, or part of one, you will need to seek the advice of a professional in order to establish the open market value at death. HMRC will require sight of the last three years of accounts and a copy of any partnership agreement.

6.12. Life policies and annuities

The open market value of a life policy (e.g., life assurance, mortgage protection, life insurance, etc.) that matures on death is the amount paid out by the provider to the estate. If the deceased owned a life policy with another, the deceased's share must be included within the death estate. If the policy is a 'joint life and survivor policy', again, the deceased's share must be included.

If the deceased is entitled to benefit from a policy on the life of another person who is still alive, the open market value is the amount for which the policy can be sold, not its surrender value.

The value of any purchased life annuities which continue after death must also be reported to HMRC.

In all instances, contact the relevant provider. They will give you the appropriate details together with guidance on values.

❖ If the deceased paid premiums on any life policies which were not for their own benefit or did not pay out to the estate, or where the deceased transferred the benefit of a policy to a third party, this may represent a gift. If so, a value must be included within the estate. Section 16.18 provides more detail on gifts generally.

❖ Ensure you have current contact details for the policy provider. The policy document may be out of date and the company name may have changed. Check on the provider's website in the first instance or contact the Financial Conduct Authority if you are struggling to make progress.

6.13. Salary and employment benefits

If the deceased was in employment at the date of death, you must notify the employer of the death in writing. Enquire whether there are any outstanding salary amounts or any other benefits due to the estate. Any value must be included within the deceased's estate.

6.14. Pensions

You must provide details of the deceased's pension entitlement to HMRC. This includes any pension arrears or refunds, guaranteed pension payments and lump sum benefits. HMRC requires this detail regardless of whether any lump sum is payable to the estate or a third party, or whether the payments are chargeable to inheritance tax or not.

The relevant pension provider will give you the appropriate details together with guidance on the values which need to be included as part of the deceased's estate.

❖ If, in the two years before death, the deceased transferred pension benefits, made a nomination, appointment or assignment, or made any changes to their pension benefits, this may represent a gift. If so, a value must be included within the estate. Contributions made by a member or employer may also be a gift if made whilst the deceased was in ill health. Section 16.18 provides more detail regarding gifts, and the pension provider or HMRC will be able to advise you further if this is in point.

❖ The age of the deceased together with their employment record, amongst other factors, will provide you with some indication of whether a pension entitlement may be due.

❖ Search through the deceased's bank statements and paperwork for clues as to the existence of a pension scheme. There may be direct payments to or from bank accounts. In addition, most pension schemes are required to send a statement every year to their members.

❖ If the deceased was employed at the time of death, contact their employer in the first instance and ask whether the deceased was a member of an occupational pension scheme and who the provider was. If this is the case, contact the scheme administrator or pension provider to establish the entitlement on death.

❖ If you suspect the deceased may have a pension entitlement through a previous employer or a personal pension scheme but are unsure of the details, try making a search application through the Pension Tracing Service. They have a database of over 200,000 workplace and personal pension schemes and the service is free.

❖ If the deceased was in receipt of a state pension, contact the Pension Service to advise of the death or use the 'Tell Us Once' scheme where available.

6.15. Taxes and benefits

The deceased's personal tax affairs up to the date of death must be finalised, with any tax repayment or additional tax due included within the value of the estate.

Notify HMRC and relevant benefits offices of the deceased's death as soon as possible. You can do this either through the 'Tell Us Once' scheme if available, by phone or post. You will need the deceased's National Insurance Number and Unique Taxpayer Reference, if available, before doing so. Full contact information is available on the government's website.

Whether you need to complete a self-assessment tax return on behalf of the deceased depends on the nature of the deceased's income. If the deceased's income was all taxed at source (e.g., a salary under PAYE), HMRC will have all the relevant details and you will not be required to provide additional information. If the deceased's tax affairs are more complex (e.g., the deceased was self-employed, a higher rate tax payer or undertook transactions which resulted in a capital gains tax liability), you will need to complete a self-assessment form. You will be advised of the appropriate course of action by HMRC.

❖ Any outstanding self-assessment tax returns will need to be completed and submitted. Consider seeking professional advice where the deceased's tax affairs are not straightforward.

❖ A repayment of tax is more likely where the deceased died earlier in the tax year and paid income tax under PAYE.

6.16. Foreign property

If the deceased's estate includes foreign property, you need to consider the foreign law relating to the property as well as the validity of any will made by the deceased. It is highly advisable to seek the guidance of a professional who is qualified to practise in the law of the relevant country. The Law Society, or appropriate foreign embassy, will be able to provide a list of suitably qualified professionals.

English law determines the location of assets. Some of the most common are as follows:

❖ Land; in the country of physical location.

❖ Debts; in the country where the non-UK resident lender or debtor resides.

❖ Shares; in the country where the share register is kept.

❖ Household goods and cash; in the country of physical location.

❖ Bank accounts; in the country where the branch is located.

The sterling value, as at the date of death, of any foreign assets owned by the deceased must be included within the deceased's estate. Foreign assets are chargeable to inheritance tax if the deceased was domiciled in the UK at the time of death.

6.17. Interests in trusts

Whether an interest in a trust should be brought into account depends on the type of trust and the date it was created. Contact the trustees in the first instance. They will provide you with guidance as to whether the trust is chargeable to inheritance tax and the value to include within the estate.

6.18. Gifts and lifetime transfers of assets

The value of any gifts or lifetime transfers made by the deceased within seven years of death must be included within their estate. There are, however, exemptions and reliefs available which may reduce or completely extinguish the value of any gifts or transfers made.

Begin by drawing up a list of all gifts or transfers made by the deceased. Any transaction which has resulted in the value of the deceased's estate going down in the seven years before death is relevant. It might include gifts of cash and assets, or the sale of a house for less than its market value. The value of the gift is the amount by which the deceased's estate decreases as a result of the transfer. Contact HMRC if you are unsure about whether to include any particular transaction or the value to apply.

Next, consider whether any exemptions or reliefs apply. Certain smaller transfers are exempt including the following:

❖ An annual exemption of £3,000 per tax year which may be carried forward to the following tax year if unused.

❖ A small gifts exemption of £250 in any one year to any individual. There is no limit to the number of gifts which may be made, however, if the gift exceeds £250 to any one individual then the full amount becomes chargeable subject to the availability of the annual exemption.

❖ Lifetime gifts that represent normal expenditure from the deceased's income. Certain criteria must be met for this exemption to apply which can be checked with HMRC.

❖ Gifts in consideration of marriage and civil partnership within specific limits. Check with HMRC regarding current limits. Any gift which exceeds the limit is chargeable subject to the availability of the annual exemption.

Other exemptions and reliefs which may apply to gifts and lifetime transfers include the spousal exemption, business property relief, agricultural property relief, and gifts to qualifying charities. We make reference to these in Chapter 10.

Gifts made 'with reservation of benefit' are a special type of gift. They arise when the recipient of a gift does not fully own it or where the deceased took some benefit from it. Any gift or transfer of this type made after 18 March 1986 must be reported to HMRC. The seven-year rule does not apply. Examples of this type of gift include where a parent transfers ownership of a home to a child but continues to live there rent free, or where a parent transfers ownership of a bank account to a child but continues to receive the interest thereon. Contact HMRC if you believe this may be in point.

❖ Discuss the potential existence of any gifts and asset transfers with relatives, friends and professional advisors of the deceased.

❖ Examine bank statements for clues of any large cash payments or regular payments made for the benefit of another individual.

❖ If, in the two years before they died, the deceased made an amendment to or disposed of their pension, consider whether a gift or transfer of value has been made.

❖ If the deceased paid premiums into a life assurance policy from which they or their estate did not benefit, or if the deceased transferred a life assurance policy to a named beneficiary within seven years of death, consider whether this might constitute a gift or transfer of value.

6.19. Debts

Debts incurred by the deceased up to the date of death are allowable deductions when calculating the value of the estate for inheritance tax purposes. Types of debt the deceased might typically owe include:

❖ Mortgages

❖ Unsecured lending including personal loans and credit cards

❖ Bank overdrafts

❖ Household and property bills, e.g., utility bills, council tax and so on.

❖ Personal taxes

❖ Rent arrears

❖ Pension overpayments

❖ Debts owed by the deceased to other individuals

❖ Care home fees

Debts may only be deducted if the deceased had received something in return as at the date of death, e.g., a bill for repainting the house is deductible provided the work was carried out prior to the deceased's death. Consider any un-cleared cheques carefully.

They are only deductible if they relate to goods or services provided to the deceased prior to death.

Funeral expenses, so long as they are reasonable, are also deductible for inheritance tax purposes. This includes the cost of a headstone, flowers and any refreshments provided for the mourners after the service.

❖ You must notify relevant creditors and suppliers of the deceased's death, confirm the amount outstanding and let them know payment may be delayed pending the receipt of a grant of representation.

Debts incurred by the personal representative whilst administering the estate (e.g., professional and valuation fees, probate fees and so on) are not an allowable expense for HMRC purposes. These expenses may, however, be reclaimed from the estate.

7. Notify organisations of the death

We have already touched upon the task of notifying organisations of the death throughout Chapter 6. Once notified, the relevant organisations will update their records and take the appropriate action as well as advising you of the procedures to be followed and forms to be completed once the grant of representation is issued. In many instances, they will also provide you with valuations for inheritance tax purposes.

❖ Notifying organisations of the death as soon as possible will help prevent identify fraud.

8. Open a personal representative bank account

There is no obligation to do so, but it is wise and advisable to open a separate bank account to deal with all monies relating to the deceased's estate. It will make the task of keeping financial records easier. Mixing your own personal finances with that of the deceased's estate may lead to errors, confusion or misunderstandings which is clearly undesirable.

The relevant bank or financial institution of your choice will direct you on the appropriate procedure for opening an account.

9. Keep financial records

It is important to maintain clear and complete financial records when administering the estate. The personal representative is accountable to beneficiaries as well as government authorities and so you must keep all receipts, invoices and supporting documentation for when you are asked to prove the numbers.

As well as valuing the estate at the date of death (as discussed in Chapter 6), you will need to keep track of monies paid and received during what is known as the administration period i.e. the time between the date of death and when you finish winding up the estate. This might include dividend or rental income, interest paid or received on a bank account, professional fees for dealing with the estate and so on.

Your records will be used as the basis for HMRC purposes, distributing the estate to beneficiaries and producing final estate accounts. The more up to date and organised you are with your paperwork, the easier it will be.

10. Calculate and pay inheritance tax

10.1. Setting the scene

By this stage in the process you will have gathered together information about the deceased's assets, debts and gifts and established their value either through your own personal research, writing to the relevant financial institution or appointing valuation experts. It is now time to consider whether any inheritance tax is due and, if so, how much.

In many cases, there will be no inheritance tax to pay after taking into account the various tax exemptions and reliefs available. However, an HMRC tax form must still be completed regardless of whether any tax is due or not. A grant of representation will not be issued without the appropriate HMRC form being submitted and any tax bill being settled.

All the forms and guidance booklets mentioned throughout this chapter are available to download from the government website.

10.2. Which HMRC form do I need to complete?

There is basically a choice of two forms to complete – a simple form (the IHT 205) or a more complex one (the IHT 400). The IHT 205 is, generally speaking, used for more straightforward, lower value estates. It only requires brief details and is sufficient for the majority of cases although cannot be used if the estate has an inheritance tax liability.

It is advisable to begin by carefully reading the IHT 205 together with the comprehensive guidance booklet IHT 206. This will alert you to the need to complete the more complex IHT 400 if required. If the IHT 400 is required, it must be completed and submitted to HMRC within 12 months of the date of death otherwise financial penalties apply. There is no deadline for the IHT 205.

The IHT 205 is now available to complete online if you are making a personal application without a professional advisor. It is through invitation only by HMRC. Contact their helpline for details, or if you have any general queries relating to the completion of the forms.

10.3. What tax reliefs and tax exemptions are available?

Reliefs and exemptions are available to potentially lower or extinguish any inheritance tax liability. The nil-rate band of £325,000 is the current tax free allowance available to all death estates. If the net estate (i.e. the sum of assets, debts and gifts) is valued at more than £325,000 there may be inheritance tax to pay on the excess unless other reliefs and exemptions are available. The more common reliefs and exemptions available are considered in outline below in order to give you an awareness.

❖ *Transfer of unused nil-rate band from a deceased spouse or civil partner.* If the nil-rate band was not used or only partially used when a first spouse or civil partner died, the unused amount can be transferred to a surviving spouse or civil partner on their death provided certain conditions are met. This means that the nil-rate band available to the estate of the surviving spouse or civil partner could be as much as doubled to £650,000. If this is relevant to the deceased's estate, you must make an application to transfer the unused nil-rate band by completing either HMRC form IHT 217 or IHT 402 depending on individual circumstances. Begin with IHT 217 and then move on to IHT 402 if you are alerted to do so. All claims must be made no later than 24 months following death.

❖ *Main residence nil-rate band, effective 6 April, 2017.* A new measure has been introduced for deaths on or after 6 April, 2017, whereby an additional nil-rate band is available when a main residence is passed on death to a direct descendant. The value of the main residence nil-rate band for an estate is the lower of the net value of the interest in the residential property (i.e. after deducting any liabilities such as a mortgage) or the maximum amount of the band. The maximum amount will be phased in as follows:

£100,000 in tax year 2017/2018

£125,000 in tax year 2018/2019

£150,000 in tax year 2019/2020

£175,000 in tax year 2020/2021

❖ *Assets passing to a spouse, civil partner or qualifying charity.* There is a general exemption from inheritance tax for assets passing between spouses, civil partners or to a qualifying charity.

❖ *Gifts exemptions and Taper relief.* There are a number of exemptions available for gifts or transfers made by the deceased in the seven years before death. Please refer back to Chapter 6 for more details. Taper relief is available to reduce any inheritance tax payable on gifts where the gift is made more than three but less than seven years prior to death.

❖ *Agricultural Property, Business Property and Woodland Reliefs.* Tax reliefs may be available where the deceased's estate includes agricultural, business or woodland assets. This is a more complex area and you should seek professional advice if this applies. Form IHT 400 will need to be completed if the estate meets the conditions for these reliefs.

10.4. Calculating inheritance tax

If there is likely to be a significant inheritance tax liability and there is a possibility of reducing the amount, we advise you to seek professional advice from a solicitor or accountant.

The calculation of inheritance tax becomes more complicated if there are tax free gifts within a will, or an exempt beneficiary (i.e. spouse, civil partner or qualifying charity) is due to inherit the residue of the estate. You should also be aware that there are rules regarding how certain reliefs and exemptions interact with each other which can prove complicated to follow.

If the position is straightforward, you can calculate the amount yourself. Alternatively, you can ask HMRC to calculate the tax on your behalf. Contact their helpline for further assistance. Details are on the government website.

10.5. Paying inheritance tax

The deadline for paying any inheritance tax liability is six months following the end of the month of death or when the IHT 400 is filed with HMRC, whichever is earlier. Interest is chargeable from this time.

You need an IHT reference number and payslip before you can make any payment and before you submit the IHT 400. In order to obtain one, fill in form IHT 422 and send it to the address shown on that form or apply online. HMRC recommend applying for an IHT reference number two weeks before sending the IHT 400, so plan ahead and give yourself enough time.

10.6. Changes to the inheritance tax calculation

The inheritance tax calculation may change after submission to HMRC as a result of a number of factors including land or shares which have been sold at less than probate value, a deed of variation or gifts to charity.

It is possible to make an application for loss relief to reduce the amount of inheritance tax payable in these circumstances. You should make sure this is the best thing to do having regard to all taxes potentially affected.

11. Apply for the grant of representation

11.1. Setting the scene

Now you know the contents and value of the deceased's estate and have completed the inheritance tax form required by HMRC, you are in a position to apply for a grant of representation. This is the legal document which confirms the authority of the personal representative to act and administer the estate. It also confirms the validity of the will or that the deceased died without leaving a will. Certain organisations need to see this document before allowing access to the deceased's assets which otherwise remain frozen.

There are three types of grant of representation, all of which are issued by one of the probate registries located throughout the country. If there is a valid will with named executors the grant is known as a 'grant of probate'. In the event that there is a valid will but no executor is named within it or none of the named executors are prepared or able to act, you will apply for a 'grant of letters of administration (with will annexed)'. Where there is no valid will the probate registry will issue a 'grant of letters of administration'.

The personal application process for applying for all three types of grant is basically the same and involves selecting a probate registry, completing an application form, assembling and providing requested supporting documentation, paying a fee and attending an interview to swear an oath.

Throughout this chapter, we refer to a number of leaflets available from HM Courts and Tribunals Services which provide practical guidance for completing the grant application. They are available to download from the government website.

11.2. Is a grant of representation always needed?

The short answer is no. Not all estates require a grant of representation. The circumstances where a grant of representation is not required include the following:

❖ *Estates with no land, property or shares.* A grant of representation is not required where the estate consists entirely of assets for which there is no legal proof of title, e.g., personal goods, personal currency and motor vehicles.

❖ *Estates of less than £5,000.* You will not normally need to register a grant of representation with organisations where an estate is valued at less than £5,000.

❖ *Certain nominated property.* Before 1 March 1981, it was possible to nominate an individual to receive certain National Savings investments and government stocks on the death of the investor. No new nominations could be made after 1 March 1981, but nominations made before this time remain valid. Investments nominated in this way do not require a grant of representation and are payable directly to the nominated individual regardless of any clause to the contrary in the deceased's will. However, HMRC confirmation that any inheritance tax bill has been paid may be required for investments of significant value.

❖ *Joint assets held as joint tenants.* A grant of representation is not required to deal with assets held jointly as joint tenants.

11.3. The application form PA1

When applying for a grant of representation, you need to complete the probate application form PA1, provide supporting documentation as indicated and send all requested documents to the correct address as instructed on the form. You must say how many copies of the grant of representation you require. This will depend on the number of organisations you have contacted which require sight of the grant. Ordering a number of copies enables you to contact several organisations at the same time and, therefore, speeds up the process generally. Copies are cheaper when ordered at the time of application.

11.4. The application fee

The current fees for grant applications and copy documents are detailed in guidance leaflet PA3 Probate Fees. You must enclose a cheque with your application.

11.5. Checking the validity of the will

If there is a will, it must meet certain legal requirements as discussed in Chapter 5. The personal representative must check that this is the case. On receipt of the grant application, the probate registrar undertakes a careful check to ensure legal requirements are met and the will is valid. The registrar may require an affidavit in a variety of circumstances to confirm certain matters. This may happen where, for instance, the attestation clause is insufficient, or where confirmation is required that alterations to the will have been duly executed. A grant of representation can be refused if the registrar is unable to conclude that the will is duly executed.

11.6. Attending interview and oaths

Once the probate registry has reviewed the grant application and is satisfied that all requirements have been met, you will be sent an oath to swear for which all applicants to the grant must attend an interview. The PA1 requires you to select the location for this.

You can select a probate venue listed on Form PA4 for which no fee is charged. Or, you may choose to use a local solicitor convenient to you (known as a 'commissioner of oaths') for which a small fee is charged. It may prove quicker to use a local solicitor as there are waiting times to secure an interview at a probate venue. Also, bear in mind that a local solicitor may be more convenient if there are several applicants attending. The interview itself should take no longer than ten minutes.

11.7. Problem areas – caveats and citations

A grant of representation can be stopped by entering a caveat. Examples of why a caveat might be entered into include doubts over the validity of the will or a dispute between persons equally entitled to apply for a grant. Form PA8 provides further details as to the process involved.

If a person is entitled to take out a grant of representation but either refuses to do so or refuses to renounce their right and be passed over, the applicant can ask for a citation. The applicant must first enter a caveat with the probate registry and then swear an affidavit confirming the circumstances.

Caveats and citations, particularly where litigation may result, are not layman's territory and a solicitor should be consulted if this is in point.

12. Collect in the assets

12.1. Setting the scene

In straightforward cases, it can typically take four weeks from the date the application is submitted to the probate registry for a grant of representation to be issued. Once you have received the grant, you must check the details and make sure they are correct as mistakes can be made. If there is an error, contact the relevant probate registry as soon as you can and ask for the document to be amended. Once this is complete, you will be in a position to gain access to, and collect in, the deceased's assets.

12.2. Registering the grant of representation

You must register the grant of representation by sending an office copy to the relevant organisations. You should keep the original in a safe place as it cannot be replaced. Once this is done, follow the procedures as laid out by the various organisations in order to collect in the assets.

Any uncashed cheques made payable to the deceased must be returned to the drawer together with an office copy of the grant of representation and a request for a replacement or amendment to the name of the personal representative's bank account. This might include dividend payments or other types of income received since the deceased's death.

12.3. Notifying beneficiaries

You may choose to let the beneficiaries know the grant of representation has been received although you are under no obligation to do so.

13. Pay debts

13.1. Setting the scene

All debts should be paid before any distributions are made. Whilst there is no specified timeframe within which debts must be settled, the personal representative is obliged to act with due diligence and ensure the interests of the estate are safeguarded. You should, therefore, direct your efforts towards paying interest bearing debts as soon as possible in order to protect the value of the estate.

13.2. I need to sell assets to pay debts – which do I sell?

There are a variety of factors you need to think about if assets must be sold to pay debts. We provide an overview below. This can be a complicated area and you should seek professional advice in the event that the estate is insufficient to meet all legacies or the tax position is complex.

❖ *The terms of the will.* The law tells us the order in which assets should be used to pay debts. Assets which form part of the residuary estate should be used first. This is followed by any assets used for general legacies. Assets relating to specific legacies are the last port of call to pay debts. A careful reading of the will is required in order to establish whether a legacy is specific or general. The key point here is that a specific legacy is separately identifiable from property of a similar type. i.e. *'I give Anne my mother's gold bracelet'* is a specific legacy as one can identify from the description exactly which bracelet we mean. *'I give Anne a gold bracelet'* is a general legacy as the testator could be referring to any gold bracelet. A gift of cash can be specific provided the description is clear enough. i.e. *'I give the £1,000 kept in a box behind the bedroom cupboard to Paul'* is a specific legacy whereas *'I give £1,000 to Paul'* is a general legacy.

❖ *The wishes of the beneficiary*. If a beneficiary has asked for a specific asset, e.g., a piece of jewellery, you should make efforts to accommodate the request where possible and treat the situation in a sensitive manner.

❖ *Tax implications*. Gains made on assets sold during the administration period by the personal representative may give rise to a capital gains tax liability. The personal representative's annual exemption for capital gains tax is the same as that of an individual and they are entitled to the annual exemption in the year of death and the following two years. The respective tax positions of the beneficiary and personal representative should be considered carefully before selling any assets to ensure the best tax position is achieved.

13.3. Payment to creditors who are bankrupt

Before you make any payment, you must make sure the creditor or supplier is not bankrupt. If a creditor is bankrupt, payment should be made either to a) the trustee in bankruptcy if an individual or b) the receiver or administrator if a company.

Undertake bankruptcy searches before paying debts if there is any doubt in your mind as to the status of the creditor. For individual creditors or sole traders, this can either be done at the Land Registry for a small charge or for free at the following web link www.gov.uk/search-bankruptcy-insolvency-register. For companies, undertake a company search at Companies House.

14. Claims and disputes against the estate

14.1. Setting the scene

We are now reaching the latter stages of administering the estate. Before we go any further, we must pause and consider whether there are any third parties who may seek to make a claim or raise a dispute against the estate. If a personal representative distributes the estate and subsequently discovers such a claim or dispute exists, they may be held personally liable for any monies payable as a result. How can you guard against this?

We now consider the different ways in which you can seek to protect yourself.

14.2. Section 27 Notice, Trustees Act 1925

After you have received the grant of representation, we recommend you put a Section 27 Notice in The London Gazette. If the deceased's estate includes a property or place of business, a Section 27 Notice should also be put in a newspaper that is local to the property or business.

Placing a Section 27 Notice ensures sufficient effort has been made to locate creditors before distributing the estate to beneficiaries and protects the personal representative from being liable for any unidentified creditors. The time limit for claims by creditors under the notice is two months and one day from the date the notice is published. You should not distribute the estate before this time period expires.

If you do not place a Section 27 Notice, and a creditor subsequently comes forward after the estate has been distributed, then you may have some personal liability for the unidentified debt.

On expiry of the time limit, any claimant must seek recovery of debts from the beneficiaries, rather than from the personal representative. This notice does not protect the personal representative from creditors who they already know of, regardless of whether the creditor responds to the notice.

Go to the London Gazette website for further details about placing a Section 27 Notice. You will need to provide an office copy of the grant of representation before placing a notice in the London Gazette. Local newspapers do not require sight of the grant of representation.

14.3.   The Inheritance (Provision for Family and Dependants) Act 1975

Anyone making a will can leave their property to whomever they choose. However, under the provisions of the Inheritance (Provision for Family and Dependants) Act 1975, certain individuals may make a claim for a reasonable share of the estate even where the deceased left them nothing or very little. The IPFDA 1975 also applies if there is no will and the estate is subject to the rules of intestacy.

Claims may be made by the following people:

❖ A spouse or civil partner.

❖ A former spouse or civil partner who has not remarried or entered into a subsequent civil partnership.

❖ A person living as a spouse or civil partner in the same household for the two years ending with death.

❖ Children, including adopted children.

❖ Anyone treated as a child of the marriage, civil partnership or family unit.

❖ Anyone who considers they were maintained to a material extent by the deceased immediately prior to death and can demonstrate that this was the case.

The time limit for claims is six months from the date of the grant of representation although this can be extended at the court's discretion depending on the circumstances. The personal representative may incur personal liability if they distribute the estate within the six-month time period and a successful application is made. They will not be liable after this six-month period expires. It is, therefore, best practice to wait for six months from the date the grant of representation is issued before distributing the estate.

If such a claim is made against the estate you should seek legal advice as this particular area is not layman's territory.

14.4. Uncertain and unknown claims

There could be a situation where a debt or liability of the estate *may* arise in the future but it is not certain. For instance, the deceased may have guaranteed the debt of a third party which may or may not be called. The personal representative should consider the following actions if this is the case, albeit each of the approaches have downsides.

❖ Set money aside. This may prove problematic if the amount is unknown and may delay distribution.

❖ Obtain an indemnity from the beneficiaries. This indemnity is only as good as the financial position of the beneficiary.

❖ Obtain insurance to mitigate the risk. This may prove difficult. The cost to the estate will be the premium.

❖ Apply to the court for direction. This will prove costly.

15. Obtain HMRC clearance

15.1. Setting the scene

The tax positon of both the deceased and the deceased's estate must be concluded before the estate can be distributed. You may need to consult an accountant or professional advisor if the position is complicated.

15.2. The deceased's tax position

Before finalising the estate, you must settle the deceased's personal tax affairs for the period up to the date of death together with any outstanding self-assessment tax returns from prior years.

15.3. The estate's tax position

During the administration period, the estate may receive income generated by the deceased's assets, e.g., bank interest, rental income and so on. This income is subject to income tax at the basic rate with no entitlement to a personal allowance. The personal representative only has a duty to report untaxed estate income to HMRC – there is no requirement to report if the only income received has already been taxed at source or has a tax credit attached.

In addition to income tax, a capital gains tax charge may arise if estate assets have been sold during the administration period. Personal representatives are currently liable to capital gains tax at the rate of 28% and are entitled to a full annual exemption for the year of death and the two following years.

A self-assessment tax return may need to be completed for the estate for each of the tax years from the date of death until the administration is complete. HMRC will advise whether a self-assessment return is required – often they may accept a more informal procedure if the estate meets certain criteria.

The personal representative may also need to complete a certificate of tax deduction, Form R185 Estate Income, for any residuary beneficiary who is entitled to the income of the estate. This form shows any income arising on their inheritance during the administration period, together with any tax paid thereon, and enables the beneficiaries to report their own income tax position correctly to HMRC.

15.4. Inheritance tax

HMRC may seek to challenge the value of estate assets or debts included within the inheritance tax forms even after the grant of representation had been issued. Once matters have been settled, the personal representative should request and complete Form IHT30 (Application for a Clearance Certificate) and obtain clearance from HMRC as to the final tax position. Be aware that the Clearance Certificate will not cover you if further assets come to light following clearance or if a deed of variation alters the final tax position.

16. Distribute the estate

16.1. Setting the scene

We have now reached the final step towards completing the administration of the estate. Below, we examine some of the areas to consider when distributing the estate to beneficiaries.

16.2. Identifying beneficiaries

The will or rules of intestacy determine who the beneficiaries are. This is subject to any response from the Section 27 Notice, as described in Chapter 14, as well as any potential claims under the Inheritance (Provision for Family and Dependants) Act 1975. It is advisable to obtain photo identification for all beneficiaries for your records.

16.3. Beneficiaries under the age of 18

Unless instructed by the will, no beneficiary under the age of 18 may receive a capital bequest. Similarly, an income bequest can only be received by an underage beneficiary if they are married or in a registered civil partnership. If this applies, any bequest should be held in the personal representative's name or arrangements should be made for the bequest to be paid into court until the beneficiary reaches the age of 18.

16.4. Beneficiaries who are bankrupt

Payments must not be made to beneficiaries who are bankrupt. You should undertake bankruptcy searches before distributing any bequests to confirm the position if you are in any doubt. This can either be undertaken at the Land Charges Registry for a small charge or for free at www.gov.uk/search-bankruptcy-insolvency-register.

Gifts should be paid to the trustee in bankruptcy if a beneficiary is bankrupt.

16.5. Beneficiaries of unsound mind

Bequests to persons of unsound mind should be paid to their deputy appointed by the Court of Protection or to their attorney.

16.6. Beneficiaries who cannot be found

Beneficiaries have up to 12 years in which to commence legal proceedings against a personal representative to recover their entitlement. It is, therefore, very important to undertake a thorough investigation to locate any missing beneficiaries. The following actions might prove fruitful.

❖ Publish a Section 27 Notice.

❖ Make enquires of the deceased's close family and friends, as well as the deceased's solicitor, accountant, stockbroker and financial advisor.

❖ Search the electoral register for the beneficiary or any member of their family who might know their whereabouts. Where relevant, use the beneficiary's maiden name as well as married name.

❖ Employ a professional genealogist or tracing service if the sum involved is large enough to justify the cost.

❖ Instruct a solicitor to pay the bequest into court or make an application to the court for direction (known as a Benjamin Order). This is a costly course of action.

16.7. Procedure for the transfer of assets

The procedure for the transfer of assets depends on the asset being distributed.

Personal and household goods do not require legal paperwork and can simply be passed over to the beneficiary.

Stocks and shares require completion of a stock transfer form. You can get these from law stationers or the relevant company registrar. If stocks and shares are held by a stockbroker, they will do this for you. In all cases, you must send an office copy of the grant of representation to the relevant organisation before any transfer can be actioned.

For land and buildings, the transfer process depends on whether the title is registered or unregistered and the capacity in which the property was owned by the deceased (i.e. jointly or in sole name). Account must also be taken of whether the property is mortgaged as the mortgage provider will require repayment of the mortgage, or transfer to the beneficiary. In all cases, it is advisable to appoint a conveyancing solicitor when dealing with the transfer of property.

16.8. By when must I distribute the estate?

A personal representative is not under any obligation to make any distribution until one year following death. The beneficiary of any cash gift (known as a 'pecuniary' legacy) is entitled to interest after this time on any amount outstanding.

16.9. Who pays the transportation costs of any legacies?

Any costs of transportation, e.g., insurance, carriage and so on, should be paid by the beneficiary unless there is a contrary intention expressed in the will.

16.10. Signed proof of receipt

A signed receipt should be obtained from each beneficiary confirming receipt of all bequests. This discharges the personal representative from liability.

16.11. Estate accounts and payment of residuary estate

Estate accounts should be prepared and signed off by the residuary beneficiaries. The purpose of estate accounts is to show how the residuary estate has been calculated. There is no set format in law for these accounts – they are simply there to 'tell the story' and describe how the estate was administered. We recommend you include the following:

❖ A cover note explaining the important facts such as details of the deceased, the grant of representation and beneficiaries.

❖ A schedule of assets and debts at the date of distribution together with details of any changes in value between death and distribution.

❖ A schedule of income received and expenses incurred during the administration period.

❖ All distributions made to beneficiaries.

We provide an example set of estate accounts in Appendix 6.

The residuary estate can be distributed once the estate accounts are approved and signed by the residuary beneficiaries. The personal representative bank account can be closed when all payments have cleared.

And finally, you must keep all paperwork and records for at least 12 years following the final distribution.

17. Appendices

Appendix 1: Useful contacts

❖ *Bankruptcy and Insolvency Register:* www.gov.uk/search-bankruptcy-insolvency-register. Perform bankruptcy searches for creditors and beneficiaries before payment or distribution.

❖ *The Bereavement Register:* www.thebereavementregister.org.uk. Stop unwanted junk mail.

❖ *Blue Cross for Pets:* www.bluecross.org.uk. Rehoming of pets.

❖ *The British Bankers' Association:* www.bba.org.uk. Provides helpful information about bank accounts in the UK.

❖ *British Government Stock (Gilts):* Computershare Investors Services PLC, The Pavilions, Bridgewater Road, Bristol, BS99 6ZW. Tel: 0370 703 0143. Claims for Government Stock formerly held on the National Savings Stock Register.

❖ *The Building Societies Association:* www.bsa.org.uk. General information about savings, mortgages and building societies.

❖ *Citizens Advice:* www.citizensadvice.org.uk. General help and advice regarding probate.

Appendix 1: Useful contacts

❖ *Companies House*: www.gov.uk/government/organisations/companies-house. Perform bankruptcy searches for companies before payment or distribution.

❖ *Driver and Vehicle Licensing Agency (DVLA):* www.gov.uk/tell-dvla-about-bereavement/overview. Information on informing the DVLA after someone has died.

❖ *Dogs Trust:* www.dogstrust.org.uk. Rehoming of pets.

❖ *Financial Conduct Authority*: www.fca.org.uk . Search for up to date details of providers of financial products.

❖ *The Institute of Chartered Accountants in England and Wales*: www.icaew.com. Find a Chartered Accountant authorised to provide probate services to the general public.

❖ *The Land Registry*: www.gov.uk/government/organisations/land-registry. Undertake Title Register searches to establish land ownership.

❖ *The Law Society*: www.lawsociety.org.uk. Find a solicitor authorised to provide probate services to the general public.

❖ *The London Gazette*: www.thegazette.co.uk. Place a Section 27 Notice, Trustees Act 1925 here.

❖ *London Stock Exchange Historic Price Service*: www.londonstockexchange.com. Obtain the historic price of quoted stocks and shares for any given date.

❖ *My Lost Account*: www.mylostaccount.org.uk. Find a lost bank, building society or NS&I account with this free online tracing service.

❖ *National Savings and Investments:* www.nsandi.com. Download Form NS&I 904 to claim any investments held by the deceased.

❖ *The National Will Register (AKA Certainty):* www.nationalwillregister.co.uk. Commercial organisation which administers a registration and search facility for wills.

❖ *Pension Tracing Service:* www.gov.uk/find-pension-contact-details. Find a lost pension with this free online tracing service.

❖ *The Post Office:* www.postoffice.co.uk. Redirection of the deceased's mail.

❖ *Principal Registry of the Family Division.* Record Keeper's Department, First Avenue House, 7th Floor, 42-49 High Holborn, Holborn, London, WC1V 6NP. Tel: 0207 421 8509. Make enquiries here if searching for the deceased's will.

❖ *RSPCA:* www.rspca.org.uk. Rehoming of pets.

❖ *Tell Us Once Scheme:* www.gov.uk/after-a-death/organisations-you-need-to-contact-and-tell-us-once. Service that allows you to report a death to most governmental agencies in one go.

❖ *UK Government:* www.gov.uk/wills-probate-inheritance. Links to HMRC and probate application and guidance forms (IHT 205, IHT 400, PA1, etc.), general advice regarding the process and a helpline for queries.

❖ *Unclaimed assets:* www.unclaimedassets.co.uk. Trace and claim missing assets in the UK.

Appendix 2: To-do list by chapter

The following represents a snapshot of the more common tasks you need to consider and complete as you administer the estate. It is designed to focus your thinking and is not necessarily comprehensive; all estates are different. More detail is provided throughout the book.

Chapter 1: Who can administer an estate?

✔

Identify the personal representative(s).

☐

Chapter 2: Plan ahead...before you begin

Consider the circumstances in which it is advisable to appoint a professional advisor and do so if necessary.

☐

Confirm whether a grant of representation is required.

☐

Confirm whether any inheritance tax is due and organise funding if required.

☐

Chapter 3: Register the death

Register the death and obtain a death certificate (including copies).

☐

Sign up to the 'Tell Us Once' scheme if available.

☐

Chapter 4: Safeguard and protect estate assets and pets

Physically secure the assets and property of the deceased. Change any locks if necessary and arrange secure storage for any portable valuables. If the deceased owned a property, turn off all utility supplies if appropriate and consider whether there is a danger of water pipes freezing at the property.

☐

Appendix 2: To-do list by chapter

Specifically search for insurance policies (including buildings and contents insurance) which are required to protect the assets and property of the estate. ☐

Check existing insurance policies are fit for purpose and amend accordingly where they fall short of requirements. Notify relevant insurers of the change in circumstances. ☐

Obtain appropriate insurance for assets which require insurance but do not have it. ☐

If the deceased had pets, ensure that suitable arrangements are in place to safeguard their welfare. ☐

Chapter 5: Establish who is entitled to inherit

If the deceased left a will, locate it, keep it physically safe and check it is valid. Make sure you fully understand its contents. If there is no valid will, apply the rules of intestacy to the estate. ☐

Chapter 6: Identify and value the estate

Undertake a thorough search of the deceased's paperwork and online affairs to identify any information that will help you to administer the estate. ☐

Obtain valuations for assets and debts of the estate as at the date of death. ☐

Collate information of any gifts made by the deceased in the seven years before death. ☐

Chapter 7: Notify organisations of the death

Notify relevant authorities of the death and cancel contracts, subscriptions, online accounts etc. Appendix 4 contains letter templates to help you with this.

Re-direct the deceased's post to the personal representative in charge of day-to-day administration. This will help prevent identify fraud.

Chapter 8: Open a personal representative bank account

Open a personal representative bank account.

Chapter 9: Keep financial records

Create worksheets to keep track of estate assets, debts, gifts and any income arising, and expenses incurred, during the administration period. See Appendix 3 for example templates.

Chapter 10: Calculate and pay inheritance tax

Complete HMRC tax form IHT 205 or IHT 400, available to download from the UK Government website.

Pay any inheritance tax due.

Chapter 11: Apply for the grant of representation

Apply for the grant of representation using Form PA1, available to download from the UK Government website.

Appendix 2: To-do list by chapter

Chapter 12: Collect in the assets

Provide a copy of the grant of representation to all relevant institutions. ☐

Collect in and realise (i.e. sell) any assets where appropriate. ☐

Chapter 13: Pay debts

Settle all outstanding debts. ☐

Chapter 14: Claims and disputes against the estate

Advertise for creditors via a Section 27 Notice. ☐

Confirm there are no claims under the Inheritance (Provision for Family and Dependants) Act 1975. ☐

Chapter 15: Obtain HMRC clearance

Finalise the deceased's tax position and that of the estate. ☐

Obtain HMRC tax clearance. ☐

Chapter 16: Distribute the estate

Produce estate accounts and distribute the estate. Appendix 6 contains sample final estate accounts. ☐

Close the personal representative bank account once all payments have cleared. ☐

Keep all paperwork for 12 years. ☐

Appendix 3: Worksheet formats

Here are some suggested templates for setting up worksheets to keep financial records.

Schedule of assets at the date of death

Description	Ownership type	Value at date of death	Realised value	Date death notified	Date grant registered

Schedule of debts at the date of death

Creditor name	Date death notified	Value	Date debt paid

Schedule of gifts

Description	Date of gift	Name of recipient	Relationship to the deceased	Value

Schedule of income and expenses arising during administration period

Description	Value	Date received or paid

Schedule of legacies

Beneficiary name	Beneficiary address	Amount or asset	Date paid or transferred

Appendix 4: Letter templates

❖ Notification of death to a bank or building society

{*Your name and address*}

{*Provider's name and address*}

{*Date of letter*}

Dear {*Sir or Madam*},

Re: The Estate of {*deceased's name*}, Account Number {*account number*}

I am the Personal Representative of {*deceased's name and address*}, an account holder of yours who died on {*date of death*}. I enclose a death certificate for your records which I would be grateful if you could return to me at your earliest convenience.

Please provide me with the following:

1. Details of all accounts held by the deceased, either in sole name or joint names, and the balances thereon as at the date of death.

2. For joint accounts, confirmation of the co-owners' details and whether the accounts were held as joint tenants or tenants-in-common.

3. Details of any interest accrued but not yet paid on all accounts as at the date of death.

4. Details of any interest paid on all accounts in the two years up to the date of death. Please state whether any tax was deducted at source and, if so, the tax amount.

5. A list of all direct debits and standing orders payable from accounts in the deceased's sole name. Please confirm these have been stopped as at the date of death.

6. Details of any mortgages or loans held by the deceased with you, either in sole name or joint names, and the balances outstanding thereon as at the date of death.

7. Details of any insurance policies held by the deceased with you.

8. A list of any documents held by you on behalf of the deceased, for example, deeds, share certificates etc.

9. Confirmation of the procedure for advancing funds from the deceased's sole accounts for the payment of funeral costs, inheritance tax and probate fees.

10. The forms which need to be completed for closing the deceased's account(s) with you.

I understand all accounts held in the sole name of the deceased will be frozen. Please confirm this has been actioned. You will be contacted separately regarding any action to be taken in respect of accounts held in joint names.

Please ensure any future correspondence is directed to me at the above address. Thank you for your assistance and I look forward to hearing from you in due course.

Yours faithfully,

{*Your name*}

❖ Notification of death to a mortgage provider

{Your name and address}

{Provider's name and address}

{Date of letter}

Dear *{Sir or Madam}*,

Re: The Estate of *{deceased's name}*, Account Number *{account number}*

I am the Personal Representative of *{deceased's name}*, who died on *{date of death}* and was the mortgage account holder for *{address of property}*. I enclose a death certificate for your records which I would be grateful if you could return to me at your earliest convenience.

Please provide me with the following:

1. A mortgage statement confirming capital and interest amounts outstanding as at the date of death.
2. Details of any life or endowment policy supporting the mortgage of which you are aware.

The grant of representation will be sent to you once issued. In the meantime, please do not undertake any enforcement action for any payment.

Please ensure any future correspondence is directed to me at the above address. Thank you for your assistance and I look forward to hearing from you in due course.

Yours faithfully,

{Your name}

Appendix 4: Letter templates

❖ **Notification of death to a pension provider**

{Your name and address}

{Provider's name and address}

{Date of letter}

Dear *{Sir or Madam}*,

Re: The Estate of *{deceased's name}*, Deceased

I am the Personal Representative of *{deceased's name and address}*, a member of the *{name of pension scheme}*, who died on *{date of death}*. I enclose a death certificate for your records which I would be grateful if you could return to me at your earliest convenience.

Please provide me with the following details:

1. The scheme type for HMRC purposes i.e. approved, unapproved or registered.

2. Any arrears due to, or overpayments to be refunded from, the estate as at the date of death.

3. The total pension amount payable in the tax year of death, both gross and net of tax, including amounts due at the date of death but not yet paid (i.e. a tax deduction certificate).

4. The relevant tax district and tax reference.

5. Any payments continuing after the date of the deceased's death, the individual to whom these payments will be made and the value of these, if any, to be included in the death estate for inheritance tax purposes.

6. Any lump sum payable as a result of the deceased's death and the value, if any, to be included in the death estate for inheritance tax purposes.

7. Any changes the deceased made to their pension provision or contributions in the two years prior to death.

8. Any entitlement the deceased's {*spouse or civil partner*} has to the pension scheme and details of how to make a claim.

Please cease any payments to the deceased's bank account with immediate effect and ensure any future correspondence is directed to me at the above address.

Thank you for your assistance and I look forward to hearing from you in due course.

Yours faithfully,

{*Your name*}

❖ Notification of death to an employer

{Your name and address}

{Employer's name and address}

{Date of letter}

Dear *{Sir or Madam}*,

Re: The Estate of *{deceased's name}*, NI Number *{NI number}*

I am the Personal Representative of *{deceased's name and address}*, an employee of *{name of employer}*, who died on *{date of death}*. I enclose a death certificate for your records which I would be grateful if you could return to me at your earliest convenience.

Please provide me with the following:

1. Details of any overpayments, or arrears due, in respect of salary and any other payments due including death in service benefits.

2. Details of gross salary payments together with any income tax deductions made for the tax year of death.

3. Confirmation of whether the deceased was a member of an occupational pension scheme and, if so, the relevant contact details.

4. The deceased's tax district and tax reference.

Please cease any payments to the deceased's bank account with immediate effect and ensure any future correspondence is directed to me at the above address. Thank you for your assistance and I look forward to hearing from you in due course.

Yours faithfully,

{Your name}

❖ **Notification of death to a life assurance provider**

{*Your name and address*}

{*Provider's name and address*}

{*Date of letter*}

Dear {*Sir or Madam*},

Re: The Estate of {*deceased's name*}, Policy Number {*Policy number*}

I am the Personal Representative of the above-named policy holder, who died on {*date of death*}. I enclose a death certificate for your records which I would be grateful if you could return to me at your earliest convenience.

Please provide me with the following:

1. Details of any other policies the deceased held with you, either in their sole name or jointly.

2. Amounts payable under any policy held by the deceased, (stating any interest separately), or the open market value of any policy held by the deceased as at the date of death for inheritance tax purposes.

3. Details of the procedure to follow for claiming monies under any policy held.

4. Confirmation of whether any monies payable under any policy held are payable to the deceased's estate or to a nominated beneficiary. Where the latter applies, please confirm the details including the start date of the policy and / or the date the policy was placed into trust for the benefit of the nominated beneficiary.

Please ensure any future correspondence is directed to me at the above address. Thank you for your assistance and I look forward to hearing from you in due course.

Yours faithfully,

{Your name}

❖ **Notification of death to a share registrar**

{Your name and address}

{Registrar's name and address}

{Date of letter}

Dear *{Sir or Madam}*,

Re: The Estate of *{deceased's name}*, *{description of shareholding}*

I am the Personal Representative of *{deceased's name and address}*, a shareholder who died on *{date of death}*. I enclose a death certificate for your records which I would be grateful if you could return to me at your earliest convenience.

Please provide me with details of the following:

1. Confirmation of the deceased's shareholding, or otherwise, as stated above.

2. The amount of any dividends due to be paid, both gross and net of tax, as at the date of death.

3. Details of any dividends paid in the two years up to the date of death.

4. *{number}* stock transfer forms.

Please cease any payments to the deceased's bank account with immediate effect and ensure any future correspondence is directed to me at the above address. Thank you for your assistance and I look forward to hearing from you in due course.

Yours faithfully,

{Your name}

❖ **Notification of death to NS&I**

{Your name and address}

{NS&I address}

{Date of letter}

Dear *{Sir or Madam}*,

Re: The Estate of *{deceased's name}*, Deceased

I am the Personal Representative of *{deceased's name and address}*, an account holder of yours who died on *{date of death}*. I enclose a completed Form NS&I 904 together with a death certificate, *{the related bank books, bonds and certificates}* *{and a certified copy of the Will}* for your records which I would be grateful if you could return to me at your earliest convenience.

Please provide me with details of the following:

1. The value of the deceased's holdings as at the date of death.

2. Details of other investments (if any) the deceased held with you.

3. *{Details of how to claim funds to meet funeral director expenses in advance of obtaining a grant of representation}*.

4. *{Details of how to claim funds to meet inheritance tax liabilities in advance of obtaining a grant of representation}*.

Please ensure any future correspondence is directed to me at the above address. Thank you for your assistance and I look forward to hearing from you in due course.

Yours faithfully,

{Your name}

❖ **Notification of death to house insurance provider**

{*Your name and address*}

{*Provider's name and address*}

{*Date of letter*}

Dear {*Sir or Madam*},

Re: The Estate of {*deceased's name*}, Policy Number {*policy number*}

I am the Personal Representative of {*deceased's name*}, the policy holder *for* {*property address*} who died on {*date of death*}. I enclose a death certificate for your records which I would be grateful if you could return to me at your earliest convenience.

Please can you:

1. Confirm whether the policy has been paid in full and the date of renewal.

2. Transfer the insurance cover into my name pending the issue of a grant of representation.

3. Let me know what further information you require in order to keep insurance cover in place.

All future correspondence should be directed to me at the above address. Thank you for your assistance and I look forward to hearing from you in due course.

Yours faithfully,

{*Your name*}

❖ Notification of death to trustees

{*Your name and address*}

{*Trust name and address*}

{*Date of letter*}

Dear {*Sir or Madam*},

Re: The Estate of {*deceased's name*}, Deceased

I am the Personal Representative of {*deceased's name and address*}, who died on {*date of death*}. I enclose a death certificate for your records which I would be grateful if you could return to me at your earliest convenience.

Please can you provide the following:

1. Confirmation (or otherwise) that the deceased was a beneficiary of the trust.

2. A copy of the trust instrument and details of the trust fund at the date of death.

3. A valuation of the deceased's share of the trust for inheritance tax purposes.

4. The gross and net income due to the estate as at the date of death.

5. Details of any payments made to the deceased in the previous two tax years up to the date of death.

Please ensure all future correspondence is directed to me at the above address. Thank you for your assistance and I look forward to hearing from you in due course.

Yours faithfully,

{*Your name*}

❖ **Notification of death for general debts**

{Your name and address}

{Supplier's name and address}

{Date of letter}

Dear *{Sir or Madam}*,

Re: The Estate of *{deceased's name}*, Account Number *{account number}*

I am the Personal Representative of *{deceased's name and address}*, who died on *{date of death}*. I enclose a death certificate for your records which I would be grateful if you could return to me at your earliest convenience.

Please let me have a final statement of account detailing amounts outstanding. No payment can be made to you until a grant of representation has been issued and the estate is in funds, so please do not undertake any enforcement action at this time.

All future correspondence should be directed to me at the above address. Thank you for your assistance and I look forward to hearing from you in due course.

Yours faithfully,

{Your name}

❖ **Notification of issue of grant of representation**

{Your name and address}

{Beneficiary's name and address}

{Date of letter}

Dear *{Name of beneficiary}*,

Re: The Estate of *{deceased's name}*, Deceased

As Personal Representative of *{deceased's name}*, I write to formally advise you that the grant of representation has been issued and you are a beneficiary of the estate. I enclose of copy for your records.

I currently anticipate finalising the administration of the estate and distributing legacies within the next *{time period}*. This is, of course, subject to any unforeseen circumstances and I will endeavour to keep you updated should any problems or issues arise.

In the meantime, please contact me if you have any queries and I will be pleased to assist.

Yours sincerely,

{Your name}

❖ **Receipt for legacy**

Receipt for Legacy

The Estate of {*deceased's name*}, Deceased

I, {*name of beneficiary*}, of {*address of beneficiary*}, acknowledge receipt from {*name of personal representative*}, the personal representative of the late {*deceased's name*}, of {*description of legacy as in the will*} in full satisfaction of my entitlement from the estate.

Signed: ....

Dated: ....

❖ Approval of estate accounts cover letter

{*Your name and address*}

{*Residuary beneficiary's name and address*}

{*Date of letter*}

Dear {*Name of residuary beneficiary*},

Re: The Estate of {*deceased's name*}, Deceased

The administration of {*deceased's name*}'s estate is now complete subject to the approval of the final estate accounts.

For this purpose, I enclose two copies of the accounts, one for you to sign and return to me once approved and the other copy for your own records. *(I have also sent copies to other relevant parties for approval.)* Once you {*and all other parties*} have approved the accounts, I will be in a position to make the final distributions due to you {*and others*}. {*For your records, I enclose a copy of the will*}.

If you have any queries regarding the final estate accounts please contact me and I will be pleased to assist.

Yours sincerely,

{*Your name*}

Appendix 5: Section 27 Notice, Trustees Act 1925 (local newspaper)

❖ **Where there is no will**

Advertisement pursuant to Section 27 to the Trustees Act 1925

{Deceased's name}, Deceased

NOTICE IS HEREBY GIVEN pursuant to Section 27 of the Trustees Act 1925 that any person having a claim against or interest in the estate of the late *{deceased's name}* of *{deceased's address}* who died on *{date of death}* and letters of administration *{with will annexed}* to whose estate were granted on *{insert date}* by the District Probate Registry at *{Registry name}* on *{date of grant}* are required to send particulars in writing of their claim to *{contact details}* by *{insert a date no less than two months and a day from the date the notice is published}* after which date the administrators of the estate, *{name of administrators}*, will distribute the estate among the persons entitled thereto and will only have regard to the claims and interests that at that date they had notice to. They shall not be liable for claims and interests in the estate for which they have not had notice.

Dated: …………………………………………………

Signed: …………………………………………………

…………………………………………………

…………………………………………………

…………………………………………………

Administrators of the Estate

❖ Where there is a will

Advertisement pursuant to Section 27 to the Trustees Act 1925

{Deceased's name}, Deceased

NOTICE IS HEREBY GIVEN pursuant to Section 27 of the Trustees Act 1925 that any person having a claim against or interest in the estate of the late *{deceased's name}* of *{deceased's address}* who died on *{date of death}* and whose will appointed *{name of executors}* to be executors of the estate are required to send particulars in writing of their claim to *{contact details}* by *{insert a date no less than two months and a day from the date the notice is published}* after which date the executors will distribute the estate among the persons entitled thereto and will only have regard to the claims and interests that at that date they had notice to. They shall not be liable for claims and interests in the estate for which they have not had notice.

Dated: ....

Signed: ....

....

....

....

Executors of the Estate

Appendix 6: Sample final estate accounts

Final Estate Accounts

The Estate of the late ABC

ABC of 15 Applegate Street, Bath died on 25 November 2015 having appointed his son, DF, and daughter, GH, to be the executors of his last will and testament dated 31 January 2010. Probate was granted by the Oxford District Probate Registry on 15 April 2016 to DF, with GH reserving the right to take out the grant.

By his will, ABC left £5,000 to each of his three godchildren, EE, FF and GG and a charitable donation of £5,000 to the RSPCA. The residue of his estate is left, after payment of debts, funeral expenses, testamentary and other expenses to his two children DF and GH.

No inheritance tax is payable in relation to the estate.

Cash Account

Assets at the date of death

15 Applegate, Bath	*(note 1)*	£200,000.00
Furniture and other personal effects		£12,500.00
Nationwide Building Society: ISA		£15,000.00
Nationwide Building Society: Current Account		£2,434.50
NS&I Premium Bonds		£5,435.00
BMW 3 series	*(note 2)*	£4,555.00
Shares in ABC plc	*(note 3)*	£1,367.56
		£241,292.06

Debts at the date of death

Funeral expenses	(£3,250.00)
Visa credit card	(£575.50)
Council tax	(£95.00)
British Gas - gas and electricity	(£157.35)
Income tax	(£558.59)
Water bill	(£67.55)
	(£4,703.99)

Cash Account continued.

Income arising during administration period

Interest received on ISA between death and closure of account	£275.00
Premium Bond prizes	£75.00
Dividends from ABC plc since death	£23.51
	£373.51

Expenses incurred during administration period

Probate fees (including grant copies, etc.)	(£220.00)
Valuation fees	(£500.00)
Section 27 Notices, Trustees Act 1925	(£185.00)
Executor expenses (travel and accommodation, death certificates)	(£455.00)
Fees incurred in connection with the sale of 15 Applegate, Bath	(£2,550.00)
	(£3,910.00)

Net estate balance for distribution	**£233,051.58**

Distribution Account

Pecuniary legacies

EE	£5,000.00
FF	£5,000.00
GG	£5,000.00
RSPCA	£5,000.00
	£20,000.00

Residue

DF (50% of the residue)	£106,525.79
GH (50% of the residue)	£106,525.79
	£213,051.58

Balance from cash account	**£233,051.58**

Notes:

1. £200,000 represents the proceeds of sale for 15 Applegate, Bath before incurring sale costs of £2,550.00. The probate value as reported to HMRC was £210,000.

2. The probate value for the BMW 3 series was £4,000. The sales proceeds of £4,555.00 achieved represents a gain of £555.00.

3. The ABC plc shares were sold during the administration period for £1367.56 and a loss of £7.44 was made compared to the probate value of £1,375.00.

We, DF, GH, EE, FF and GG, approve and agree the accounts and will accept the amounts listed within in full satisfaction of all claims against the estate and the executors of the will.

Signed by DF   **Date**

....

Signed by GH   **Date**

....

Signed by EE   **Date**

....

Signed by FF   **Date**

....

Signed by GG   **Date**

....

18. Glossary

Administration period: the period from the date of death until the estate is wound up.

Administrator: the person specifically appointed to sort out the affairs of a person who has died intestate or without having appointed executors who are willing to act.

Administering an estate: all the tasks involved with sorting out the affairs of the deceased.

Affidavit: a declaration in writing made under oath before a person authorised to administer oaths.

Assets: any property owned by the deceased, e.g., house, money, cars and so on.

Attestation clause: a clause that is appended to a will below the place of the testator's signature demonstrating that the formalities relating to witnesses have been met.

Beneficiary: a person or other organisation entitled to inherit assets or property.

Bequest: a gift of property in a will.

Chattels: moveable property including cars, jewellery, furniture and so on.

Codicil: a formal document that amends, rather than replaces, a will and is read together with the will.

Debts: something that is owed, such as money, goods or services.

Deceased: the person who has died.

Deed of variation: a legal document required when the beneficiaries of the will or intestacy rules wish to change who inherits the estate.

Devisee: a person to whom land or buildings is gifted in a will.

Estate: all assets owned and debts owed by the deceased at the date of death. For inheritance tax purposes, an estate also includes any gifts made by the deceased within the seven years before death, as well as any gifts made from which the deceased continued to benefit.

Executor: the person specifically appointed in a will to sort out the affairs of the deceased.

Gift: a transfer of assets.

Grant of representation: the legal document which confirms the authority of the personal representative to act and administer the estate. It also confirms the validity of the will or that the deceased died without leaving a will. If the deceased left a will with named executors who are prepared and willing to act, the legal document is known as a grant of probate, otherwise it is a grant of letters of administration.

HMRC: a department of the UK government responsible for collecting taxes.

Intermeddling: undertake an act in relation to the deceased's estate which shows an intention to act as an executor or apply for probate.

Intestacy rules: the law which governs to whom a person's estate is distributed if they do not leave a valid will or the will they leave does not cover their entire estate.

Intestate: not having made a valid will or someone who dies without a valid will.

Issue: the descendants of a person i.e. children, grandchildren or remoter lineal descendants. Includes adopted children and those born either within or outside marriage.

Joint tenants: a form of joint ownership under English law whereby the deceased's share of the property automatically passes to the survivor regardless of any clause in their will or the intestacy rules.

Legacy: a gift in a will of money or personal property.

Legatee: a person who receives a gift under a will.

Minor: a person who is under the age of 18.

Nil-rate band: the value of the net estate below which no inheritance tax is due.

NS&I: National Savings and Investments

Office copy: an official copy of a document issued by the probate registry which is as valid as the original document.

Open market value: the measure used for valuing an estate for inheritance tax purpose. It represents the realistic selling price at the date of death and not, for instance, insurance or replacement value.

Pecuniary legacy: a gift of cash made in a will.

Personal representative: those individuals given the authority to wind up the affairs of someone who has died – they can either be administrators or executors.

Predeceased: to die before.

Probate registry: Probate offices that issue grants of probate and grants of letters of administration. The Principal Probate Registry is situated in Central London, and there are 11 District Probate Registries and 18 Probate Sub-Registries. These are administered by HM Courts Service, which is part of the Ministry of Justice.

Qualifying charity: a charity established in the EU (or other specified country) which a) would qualify as a charity under the law of England and Wales, b) is regulated as a charity in the country of establishment (if appropriate) and c) has mangers who are fit and proper persons to be managers of the charity.

Registered land: Land and buildings which are registered with HM Land Registry.

Renounce: in the context of being an executor, refusing the right to take on the role of executor.

Reserve power: in the context of being an executor, delaying the decision about whether to take on the role of executor.

Residuary devisee: a beneficiary who is gifted land or buildings which form part of the residuary estate.

Residuary legatee: a beneficiary who is bequeathed a gift which forms part of the residuary estate.

Residue or residuary estate: the part of the estate which remains after the payment of all funeral and legal expenses, debts and legacies.

Revocation or revoke: cancellation or cancel.

Tax year: a year which runs from 6 April to 5 April.

Tenants-in-common: a form of joint ownership under English law whereby the deceased's share passes under the terms of their will or intestacy rules.

Testator: male form of the name given to a person making a will.

Testatrix: female form of the name given to a person making a will.

Title: Ownership.

Unregistered land: Land and buildings which are not registered with HM Land Registry.

Void: being null and completely without legal force or binding effect.

Will: a written direction and instruction by which a person expresses their requirements and wishes for the distribution of their estate upon death.

Printed in Great Britain
by Amazon